Kate Chopin's

The
Awakening

Text by
Debra Geller Lieberman
(J.D., New York University School of Law)
(M.S. Ed., Hunter College)

Dr. M. Fogiel
Chief Editor

Illustrations by
Zina Parubchenko

Research & Education Association

What **MAXnotes**® *Will Do for You*

This book is intended to help you absorb the essential contents and features of Kate Chopin's *The Awakening* and to help you gain a thorough understanding of the work. The book has been designed to do this more quickly and effectively than any other study guide.

For best results, this **MAXnotes** book should be used as a companion to the actual work, not instead of it. The interaction between the two will greatly benefit you.

To help you in your studies, this book presents the most up-to-date interpretations of every section of the actual work, followed by questions and fully explained answers that will enable you to analyze the material critically. The questions also will help you to test your understanding of the work and will prepare you for discussions and exams.

Meaningful illustrations are included to further enhance your understanding and enjoyment of the literary work. The illustrations are designed to place you into the mood and spirit of the work's settings.

The **MAXnotes** also include summaries, character lists, explanations of plot, and section-by-section analyses. A biography of the author and discussion of the work's historical context will help you put this literary piece into the proper perspective of what is taking place.

The use of this study guide will save you the hours of preparation time that would ordinarily be required to arrive at a complete grasp of this work of literature. You will be well prepared for classroom discussions, homework, and exams. The guidelines that are included for writing papers and reports on various topics will prepare you for any added work which may be assigned.

The **MAXnotes** will take your grades "to the max."

Dr. Max Fogiel
Program Director

Contents

Section One: *Introduction* 1

   The Life and Work of Kate Chopin 1

   Historical Background 2

   Master List of Characters 3

   Summary of the Novel 4

   Estimated Reading Time 6

**Each Chapter includes List of Characters,
Summary, Analysis, Study Questions and
Answers, and Suggested Essay Topics.**

Section Two: *The Awakening* 7

   Chapter I 7

   Chapter II 11

   Chapter III 13

   Chapter IV 16

Chapters V and VI 19
Chapter VII 23
Chapter VIII 27
Chapter IX 29
Chapter X 33
Chapter XI 37
Chapter XII 39
Chapter XIII 41
Chapter XIV 45
Chapter XV 46
Chapter XVI 50
Chapter XVII 53
Chapter XVIII 56
Chapter XIX 59
Chapter XX 63
Chapter XXI 66
Chapter XXII 68
Chapter XXIII 71
Chapter XXIV 75
Chapter XXV 77
Chapter XXVI 81
Chapter XXVII and XXVIII 84
Chapter XXIX 88
Chapter XXX 90
Chapter XXXI 93
Chapter XXXII 95

v

Chapter XXXIII 99

Chapter XXXIV 102

Chapter XXXV 105

Chapter XXXVI 107

Chapter XXXVII 112

Chapter XXXVIII 115

Chapter XXXIX 118

Section Three: *Sample Analytical Paper Topics* 123

Section Four: *Bibliography* 127

SECTION ONE

Introduction

The Life and Work of Kate Chopin

Kate Chopin was born Katie O'Flaherty in 1850 in St. Louis to an Irish father and a French mother. Her father died in a train crash in 1855. Kate was taught and greatly influenced by her maternal great-grandmother who was an independent, free thinker. She taught Kate through storytelling, in both English and French. Additionally, Kate attended the prestigious Sacred Heart Academy, which promoted intelligence and independent thinking. Kate began her lifelong love of reading and writing there.

In 1861 the Civil War began, and Kate, after ripping down a Union flag posted in front of her home, became known as St. Louis "Littlest Rebel." During the course of the war, Kate lost her brother, her great-grandmother, and her best friend. She later wrote war stories about loss, grief, terror, and fear. She became preoccupied with death.

Kate graduated in 1868 and "came out" to the debutante scene where she was praised for her beauty and cleverness. She, however, hated the life that took her away from reading, writing, and thinking, and she particularly hated the constricting clothes that society women were forced to wear. Despite her inner rebelliousness, she married Oscar Chopin in 1870, moved to New Orleans, and had six children. She loved her husband and children but felt engulfed by her life. She became well known for taking long solitary walks (which scandalized the townspeople).

Oscar died in 1882, and Kate had an affair with a married man named Albert Sampite who later appeared in many of her major works as a character called "Alcee." She moved back to St. Louis in

1884, and after her mother died in 1885, Kate took up writing more seriously. Her publishing debut came in 1889 with a poem titled "If It Might Be." Her first novel, titled *At Fault*, was published in 1890, but national recognition did not come until her first national publication in 1894, a collection of short stories titled *Bayou Folk*.

Kate's favorite writer was Guy de Maupassant, and like him, much of Kate's fiction was considered scandalous. Nobody, however, denied her talent. She was a prolific and much published writer; she wrote short stories, poems, essays, and novels. Even the bad reviews for *The Awakening* did not hurt Kate's literary reputation. In 1900 she was included in the first edition of *Who's Who in America*, and she continued to have many admirers. However she was deeply wounded by the negative reviews and by people's lack of understanding. She wrote less often after that. Kate died in 1904 after spending the day at the St. Louis World's Fair.

Kate Chopin was a woman ahead of her time. In the 1960s, with the advent of feminism, Kate Chopin was resurrected, and *The Awakening* is considered to be one of the first feminist books.

Historical Background

Kate Chopin grew up in violent, turbulent times. She came from a slaveholding family in a city that was a major center for slave trade. There was constant fighting in St. Louis over secession. The Civil War began in 1861 when she was 11 years old, and she and everyone she knew lived in constant terror. There were times when she was confined to her home because of the fighting in the street. She learned to be self-sufficient from an early age.

After the Civil War ended, a period of strong activism among St. Louis women began. There were many outspoken suffragists, and other women who were beginning to question the path of marriage and motherhood. Susan B. Anthony was traveling and speaking extensively about equality and women's rights. By the 1890s there were many "New Women" making their way in St. Louis. These were single women who became doctors, lawyers, and journalists.

Additionally, the works of Darwin, Spencer, and Huxley were transforming intellectual thought. People were beginning to question things they had always held as truth, including definitions of morality. Finally, the Industrial Revolution was well under way, and the whole world was changing. *The Awakening* was published in 1899, just at the turn of the century, and there was constant tension between tradition and movement, old and new.

The majority of the reviews for *The Awakening* were unfavorable. Although her writing was praised, the book was described as "unhealthy," "unwholesome," "unpleasant," and "a dangerous specimen of sex fiction." Despite the fact that many women had begun to write novels with daring themes by the time *The Awakening* was published, for example, Charlotte Perkins Gilman, even novels with the most radical themes still tended to promote traditional values and have traditional resolutions. Even some of the most radical women still thought that sexual passion was immoral and unhealthy for women. So it is no surprise that even amidst the incredible changes, for women and the country as a whole, Kate Chopin was censured for the choices made by her protagonist, Edna Pontellier. Edna's passion was described by one reviewer as an "ugly, cruel, loathsome monster."

Kate Chopin, herself, and through Edna Pontellier, questioned the traditional idea of woman as wife and mother, without passion and without her own mind. *The Awakening* depicts the powerful "cage of convention" and the futility both Kate and Edna felt in trying to live a life of freedom.

Master List of Characters

Edna Pontellier—*The protagonist of the novel, she is a 28-year-old married woman with children who yearns for more out of life. The novel is about her journey of discovery.*

Leonce Pontellier—*Edna's husband; He is, by all accounts, a good man, but he treats Edna like a possession rather than an equal.*

Madame Lebrun—*The owner of the resort at Grand Isle where the Pontellier family spends their summers.*

Robert Lebrun—*The 26-year-old son of Madame Lebrun; He and Edna fall in love.*

Adele Ratignolle—*A friend of Edna's; She is a beautiful woman who is devoted to her husband and children. She is pregnant and gives birth during the book.*

Mademoiselle Reisz—*A loner at Grand Isle, she is a gifted pianist who becomes very close to Edna.*

The Farival Twins—*Two young guests at Grand Isle who play the piano for the entertainment of the other guests.*

Monsieur Farival—*Grandfather of the twins.*

Raoul and Etienne—*The Pontellier's two young children.*

Victor Lebrun—*The younger brother of Robert.*

Mariequita—*A "mischievous," carefree Spanish girl who works at Grand Isle.*

The Lovers—*A young, unmarried couple who are oblivious to all but themselves.*

Celestine—*The Pontellier's servant.*

Baudelet—*An old sailor who takes people by boat to Mass at Cheniere Caminada.*

Madame Antoine—*A fat village woman at Cheniere Caminada whose house Edna stays in when she feels ill.*

Tonie—*The son of Madame Antoine.*

Dr. Mandelet—*A good doctor who tries to help Edna.*

Alcee Arobin—*A young man-about-town with whom Edna has an affair.*

The Highcamps and the Merrimans—*Society people who are friends of Edna's.*

The Colonel—*Edna's father.*

Miss Mayblunt and Gouvernail—*Guests at Edna's dinner party.*

Summary of the Novel

The Awakening begins in Grand Isle, where the Pontellier family is vacationing for the summer. Leonce Pontellier's newspaper reading has been interrupted by the loud talking of the caged parrot so he returns to his own cottage. Edna Pontellier returns from bathing in the ocean with Robert Lebrun, and her husband criticizes her for bathing so late in the day. She and Robert share laughs over something that happened at the ocean, but Leonce is bored with the conversation. He leaves to go to a men's club at a hotel called Klein's. Robert stays with Edna.

When Mr. Pontellier returns late that night, he reprimands Edna for her neglect of the children. She begins to cry, feeling an "indescribable oppression." The next day we meet Adele Ratignolle, who is pregnant and a classic "mother-woman." Edna, Adele, and Robert spend the afternoon together, and Robert is very attentive to Edna; they later go swimming together.

At the ocean with Adele, Edna remembers the times she was in love and how she "accidentally" married Leonce. Adele warns Robert to stay away from Edna. Some weeks later, all the summer guests gather together for an evening's entertainment. We are introduced to Edna's love of music. At the end of the evening, everyone goes swimming and Robert walks Edna home. Later Edna defies Leonce and stays out in the hammock after he instructs her to go inside.

The next day Edna and Robert go to Mass together at Cheniere Caminada and spend the whole day together there. Some time later Robert announces that he is leaving for Mexico that night, and Edna tries to hide her feelings, from herself as much as from anyone else. After he is gone, she misses him very much.

At the beach one day, Edna tells Adele that although she would give her life for her children, she wouldn't give herself. Adele doesn't understand.

After the summer, they go home to New Orleans, and Edna starts to forego her usual social engagements, for which she is reprimanded by Leonce. She begins taking long, solitary walks. She has lost interest in her home and family and takes up painting. She visits Mademoiselle Reisz and reads a letter from Robert, which makes her cry.

Leonce is worried about his wife and talks to Dr. Mandelet who advises him to let her have her way and maybe it will pass. After Edna's father comes to stay for a while, Leonce and the children go away, and Edna is happily left alone. She paints, reads, and visits with friends. One of her new friends is Alcee Arobin, who is known for being a womanizer. They often go to the track together, and begin to spend time alone together in the evening.

While her family is still away, Edna decides to move out of her house to a smaller one around the corner. One day she goes to visit Mademoiselle Reisz and learns that Robert is coming home; she admits that she loves him. That night she begins her affair with Alcee Arobin and says of his kiss, "It was the first kiss of her life to which her nature had really responded." Later she is disappointed that the response wasn't brought on by love. The night before she moves, Edna has a dinner party, and Alcee stays the night.

One day Edna goes to visit Mademoiselle Reisz and finds Robert there. She is hurt that he has not called on her since his return. He dines with her at her house that night but does not call or come visit after that. She spends more and more time with Alcee, although she still longs for Robert.

Luckily Edna runs into Robert accidentally, and he goes to her home with her. They finally both declare their love, and kiss, but then Edna has to leave to be with Adele Ratignolle, who is giving birth. When she returns, Robert is gone.

The novel ends with Edna leaving New Orleans and going back to Grand Isle. Shortly after her arrival there, she swims out as far as she can into the ocean, with no strength left to return.

Estimated Reading Time

The average reader should be able to complete *The Awakening* in four to five hours. The short chapters make it easier to read, and certain chapters can be grouped together to aid the reader in understanding the story.

Chapters I through VI take place in Grand Isle and introduce the major conflicts of the novel and set the tone for Edna's awakening.

Chapters VII through XVI are the remaining chapters that take place in Grand Isle. Here we see Edna's various awakenings set in motion.

Chapters XVII through XXX take place in New Orleans. Here we see significant growth in both Edna's rebellion and her resulting conflicts.

Chapters XXXI to XXXVIII also take place in New Orleans and are about Edna's independence.

Chapter XXXIX should be read alone. The story moves back to Grand Isle, and it is the resolution of the novel.

The Awakening

Chapter I

New Characters:

Edna Pontellier: *the protagonist of the novel; a 28-year-old married woman with children who yearns for more out of life; the novel is about her journey of discovery*

Leonce Pontellier: *Edna's husband; by all accounts, a good man, but treats Edna like a possession rather than an equal*

Madame Lebrun: *the owner of the resort at Grand Isle where the Pontellier family spends their summers*

Robert Lebrun: *the 26-year-old son of Madame Lebrun; falls in love with Edna*

The Farival Twins: *two young guests at Grand Isle who play the piano for the entertainment of the other guests*

Raoul and Etienne: *the Pontellier's two young children*

Summary

Leonce Pontellier is seated in the main building (known as the "House") of a resort on Grand Isle. He is attempting to read a newspaper but is interrupted by the noise of a green and yellow parrot that speaks French and Spanish. He leaves the House and proceeds to his own cottage, where he again picks up his newspaper. He hears lots of noise from the House, including the Farival twins playing the piano, and Mrs. Lebrun, the owner of the resort. He sees his two children, ages four and five, with their quadroon nurse.

Leonce lights up a cigar and sees his wife Edna walking up to the cottage with Robert Lebrun. He reprimands them for bathing in the heat, and gives back her wedding rings, which she had taken off prior to going to the beach. Edna and Robert begin laughing about some adventure they had at the beach and try to relate it to Leonce, but he is obviously bored. Finally, he gets up and leaves for Klein's Hotel to play billiards. He invites Robert, but Robert says he would rather stay with Edna.

Edna inquires whether Leonce will be home for dinner, but he does not answer because it depends on what he finds at Klein's. Edna understands and says good-bye. Leonce promises to bring home bonbons and peanuts for the children.

Analysis

Chopin begins with an image that is very strong in women's fiction: that of a caged bird, which is "tamed for the amusement of the household." Leonce Pontellier "had the privilege of quitting their society when they ceased to be entertaining." He also exercises this privilege with his wife, whom he leaves when he is bored.

The bird's speech is also symbolic here. It imitates very well, repeating phrases it has heard but also speaks a language that nobody understands. Edna fights against being forced simply to mimic the life every other woman leads, but it is questionable whether anybody will understand her if she stops that mimicking. Still Chopin is preparing us for Edna's journey of self-discovery.

Chopin uses a bit of foreshadowing, although very few people today would pick it up. It is in the Farival twins' duet from *Zampa*. *Zampa* is an opera that records a romantic death at sea.

Chopin makes the relationship between Edna and Leonce quite clear from the beginning. After reprimanding her for bathing in the heat, Leonce looks at Edna "as one looks at a valuable piece of personal property which has suffered some damage." In contrast, Edna and Robert's relationship seems to be based on mutual affection; they have adventures and laugh together.

Study Questions

1. What kind of bird is hung in the cage?
2. Why does Leonce return to his own cottage?
3. What are the Farival twins doing at the main house?
4. Who is Edna bathing with?
5. How does Leonce look at Edna when she returns?
6. What does Leonce give to Edna upon her return?
7. What are Edna and Robert laughing about?
8. Where is Leonce going to spend the evening?
9. Why doesn't Robert go with him?
10. Does Leonce keep his promise to the children?

Answers

1. A green and yellow parrot is hung in the cage.
2. Leonce returns to his own cottage because the bird's talking was making it difficult for him to read his newspaper.
3. They are playing a duet from *Zampa* on the piano.
4. Edna is bathing with Robert Lebrun.
5. Leonce looks at Edna as if she were a valuable piece of personal property that had suffered some damage.
6. He gives Edna back her wedding rings, which she had taken off prior to bathing.
7. They are laughing about an adventure they had in the water.
8. He is going to spend the evening at the Klein's Hotel.
9. Robert prefers to stay with Edna.
10. No. He forgets the bonbons and peanuts.

Suggested Essay Topics

1. Describe the attitude of Leonce toward Edna and how it differs from Robert's.

2. What is the symbolism of the caged parrot?

Chapter II

Summary

The chapter begins with a description of Edna Pontellier. She has bright yellowish brown eyes and hair, and her eyebrows are a shade darker. She is handsome rather than beautiful, wears a frank expression, and has an engaging manner. Additionally, there is depth to her eyes and a subtlety to her features.

Robert Lebrun is also described for the reader. He is smoking a cigarette because he cannot afford cigars, although he has one that Leonce Pontellier had given to him. He is clean shaven and similar in complexion to Edna.

Robert and Edna chat together about their adventure in the water, and everything that is going on around them, including the children who are playing croquet and the Farival twins. They also talk about themselves and are both very interested in what the other has to say. Robert talks about his long-held desire to go to Mexico and make his fortune and how he remembers Grand Isle when there was no need for guests.

Edna talks about her childhood and her home in Kentucky. She reads a letter from her sister and Robert asks many questions about the family. Finally it is time to dress for dinner. Edna realizes Leonce won't be coming home, and Robert agrees because there were many club men over at Klein's. Robert then plays with the Pontellier children until dinner is ready.

Analysis

The physical description of Edna Pontellier is a clue to her character and the journey she will undertake. Her eyes look at things as if "lost in some inward maze of contemplation of thought." Her eyes have depth, and there is subtlety to her features. She is clearly not an ordinary woman. There is something deep going on inside her, some inner searching. The fact that she is handsome rather than beautiful gives a masculine edge to her and, in fact, her journey takes her into a world that had previously been exclusively male.

Robert, on the other hand, is described as a callow youth on whose face "rested no shadow of care." It is obvious that he is no match for her. Still Chopin makes it clear that they have an easy-going friendship and that they truly enjoy one another's company. This is in direct contrast to Edna's relationship with her husband. For example, Leonce doesn't come home for dinner, because he would rather be with the men at Klein's.

Chopin also introduces another characteristic that sets Edna apart from her peers. She is clearly American, and any French ancestry has been "lost in dilution." Her husband, as well as all the guests at Grand Isle, are French Creole. They have a different set of norms, values, and customs than those with which she grew up.

Study Questions

1. How does Edna look at objects?

2. How does Edna's appearance differ from other women?

3. What about Robert's appearance makes him seem immature?

4. Why does Robert smoke cigarettes?

5. How do we see the intimacy between Robert and Edna at this point?

6. Why does Robert want to go to Mexico?

7. Why does Madame Lebrun take in guests?

8. How is Edna's background different from the other guests at Grand Isle?

9. What is Edna's sister doing in the East?

10. Why does Robert assume Leonce wouldn't be coming home for dinner?

Answers

1. She looks at them as if she were lost in contemplation or thought.

2. Edna is handsome rather than pretty.

3. He is clean shaven and has no shadow of care.

4. He smokes cigarettes because he can't afford cigars.

5. They both chat incessantly and each is interested in what the other has to say.

6. He wants to make his fortune there.

7. She needs to so she can keep up her easy, comfortable lifestyle.

8. She is truly American, and any French has been lost in dilution. The other guests are all French Creole.

9. She is engaged to be married.

10. He assumes that because there were a good many New Orleans clubmen over at Klein's.

Suggested Essay Topics

1. What does Edna's appearance tell us about her personality?

2. How does Edna and Robert's relationship differ from Edna and Leonce's thus far?

Chapter III

Summary

Leonce returns from Klein's at eleven o'clock that evening, in high spirits and very talkative. Edna, who was sleeping when he came in, only half answers him as he talks. Leonce finds her lack of interest very discouraging.

Leonce forgot the bonbons and peanuts for the children, but he goes into their room to check on them. He reports back to Edna that Raoul has a fever and needs looking after. Then he sits down and lights up a cigar. Edna responds that Raoul went to bed perfectly well.

Leone reprimands Edna for her neglect of the children, reminding her that it is a mother's place to look after them. He is busy with his business and cannot do both. Edna gets out of bed to check on the children and then refuses to answer Leonce when he questions her upon her return. Leonce finishes his cigar and goes to sleep.

Edna begins to cry and slips outside to rock in the wicker chair.

It is past midnight and very quiet, except for the sounds of an old owl and, of course, the sea, which "broke like a mournful lullaby upon the night." Edna now begins crying very hard, and becomes filled with a sense of oppression and anguish. If not for the mosquitos biting her, she might have sat and cried for half the night.

Leonce is up early the next morning, ready and eager to go back to the city until the following weekend. A few days later a box of delicacies arrives from Leonce, which Edna shares with everyone. The Grand Isle ladies declare that Leonce is the best husband in the world, and Edna "was forced to admit that she knew of none better."

Analysis

We are introduced in this chapter to the assigned gender roles Edna is trying to break free of. When Leonce comes home from Klein's, he tells Edna that Raoul is sick and needs looking after. Then he sits down and lights a cigar. It is clearly not his role to take care of the children. He makes this even more clear when he reprimands Edna for her inattention and says "If it was not a mother's place to look after children, whose on earth was it?" This becomes one of the central conflicts of the novel: Edna's love for her children versus her desire for independence.

Later, when Edna goes outside to cry, the sea as symbol is brought in again. All is quiet except for an owl and "the everlasting voice of the sea. . . like a mournful lullaby." The sea is constant and eternal and speaks to Edna. In this case, it is mirroring her sadness, since a "mournful lullaby" is a song that would be sung by a sad mother.

We see the beginning of Edna's change here because she is surprised by her tears. She says that such experiences, meaning Leonce's reprimand, were not uncommon yet she was reacting differently. She was filled with "an indescribable oppression" and a "vague anguish." This is the first sign of her "awakening," although she does not yet recognize it as such.

When Leonce sends Edna a box of delicacies from the city, she is "forced" to admit to the admiring ladies that she knows of no better husband. This is one of the forces that dooms Edna's journey.

Leonce is just as he should be by society's standards; thus, Edna's desired change must confront not only her husband but society as a whole.

Study Questions

1. Why does Edna have trouble talking to Leonce when he comes home from Klein's?
2. What does Leonce do after he tells Edna that Raoul has a fever?
3. What is Leonce's opinion of raising children?
4. Why is Edna so upset after she checks on Raoul?
5. What does the sea sound like when Edna goes outside?
6. What is different about this particular argument with Leonce that causes Edna to cry?
7. What does Edna feel while she cries?
8. Is Edna upset about the fact that she is crying?
9. What does Leonce send to Edna while he is away?
10. Is Leonce considered a good husband?

Answers

1. Edna had been asleep when Leonce came in; he wakes her up.
2. He sits down to smoke a cigar.
3. He believes that it is solely the mother's responsibility.
4. She feels bad because Leonce was right, and Raoul had a fever.
5. It sounds like a mournful lullaby.
6. Edna doesn't know why she is crying, but something is changing inside her.
7. She feels an indescribable oppression and a vague anguish.
8. No. She is enjoying her solitary cry.

9. Leonce sends a box of delicacies from New Orleans.

10. Yes. All the ladies admire him and even Edna is forced to admit she knows of none better.

Suggested Essay Topics

1. What does Edna's cry and accompanying feelings suggest about her "awakening"?

2. Why is it actually a problem for Edna that Leonce is considered to be such a good husband?

Chapter IV

New Character:

Adele Ratignolle: *a friend of Edna's; a beautiful woman who is devoted to her husband and children; she is pregnant*

Summary

This chapter begins with a description of Edna's mothering. Leonce cannot define exactly Edna's failings in this regard, but as an example, if one of the Pontellier children fell, he would not rush to his mother's arms for comfort. Edna is not a "mother-woman": a breed who idolize their children and worship their husbands and have no selves of their own.

One such mother-woman is Adele Ratignolle, who is described as "the embodiment of every womanly grace and charm." She is very fond of Edna and is with her, doing her usual sewing, the day the box of delicacies arrives from Leonce. She had brought a pattern for Edna to cut for a winter outfit for the children. Edna is not interested in doing this but so as not to offend Adele, she cuts the pattern.

Edna offers Adele some bonbons, which Adele takes with some misgiving because she is pregnant. Adele had been married seven years and had a baby every two years. Robert, who is there also, tries to reassure Adele about the bonbon, but Edna blushes when he mentions the pregnancy.

Everyone at Grand Isle that summer is a Creole; Edna is a Creole only by marriage and does not feel entirely comfortable among them. She is especially taken by their freedom of expression and absence of prudery, which nonetheless went hand in hand with a strict chastity. She is embarrassed by Adele's description of a particularly difficult childbirth and by the plot of a book that everyone else had read and discussed openly.

Analysis

Here we see the contrast between Edna, who is seeking independence, and Adele Ratignolle, who is a classic "mother-woman." These mother-women "idolized their children, worshipped their husbands, and esteemed it a holy privilege to efface themselves as individuals and grow wings as ministering angels." Adele's physical description goes along with this. There is nothing subtle about Adele. She is beautiful, feminine, and maternal. In fact, her hands are never more beautiful than when she is sewing. Physically, as tempermentally, she is in direct contrast to Edna.

Adele has had a baby every two years since her wedding and is pregnant again. Chopin points out that although she is not showing yet, everyone knows she is pregnant because Adele talks about it constantly. Because Adele as mother-woman has no identity beyond wife and mother, it is crucial to her that her pregnancy is known.

Finally Edna's alienation from Creole society is brought out. She blushes when Robert talks about Adele's pregnancy and was shocked by a racy book that everyone else had read and discussed openly. This openness is in contrast to Edna's strict, moralistic upbringing.

Study Questions

1. What is given as an example of Edna's lack of mothering?

2. What is a "mother-woman"?

3. Who is considered a classic mother-woman?

4. What are three differences between Adele and Edna's appearances?

5. When are Adele's hands considered most beautiful?

6. Why did Edna cut a pattern for winter clothes for her children?

7. How do Edna and Robert know that Adele is pregnant again?

8. Why does Edna blush when Robert tells Adele it is safe to eat a bonbon?

9. Why doesn't Edna feel entirely comfortable at Grand Isle?

10. According to Edna, what is the most distinguishing characteristic of the Creoles?

Answers

1. If one of the children falls while at play, he does not rush to his mother's arms for comfort.

2. A mother-woman is a woman who idolizes her children, worships her husband, and considers it a privilege to lose her own identity.

3. Adele Ratignolle is considered a classic mother-woman.

4. (1) Edna's features are subtle and have depth while there is nothing subtle or hidden about Adele's beauty; (2) Edna's body is lean and symmetrical while Adele's is plump and (3) Edna is handsome rather than beautiful while Adele is like a bygone heroine of romance or the fair lady of our dreams.

5. They are most beautiful when they are busy sewing.

6. She does it so as not to insult Adele.

7. They know because she talks about her "condition" constantly.

8. Edna is not used to people talking about pregnancy so openly.

9. Everyone there is a Creole except Edna.

10. To Edna the most distinguishing characteristic of the Creoles is their absence of prudery.

Suggested Essay Topics

1. How does Edna's desire for independence conflict with the image of the mother-woman?

2. Compare and contrast Edna and Adele with respect to physical appearance and temperament.

Chapters V and VI

Summary

In Chapter V, Adele continues to sew, while Edna and Robert sit idle, exchanging occasional words and glances that suggest intimacy. Every summer Robert devotes himself to one woman, and this summer it is Edna. The summer before it was Adele, and they joked a bit about it as Robert described his passion to Edna. It was understood that his words of love were not to be taken seriously. Edna is glad Robert does not speak that way to her.

Edna has her sketchbook with her and begins to draw Adele. Robert praises the work, but Edna crumples it up because it does not look like Adele. While Edna is drawing, Robert rests his head against her arm. Even after she pushes him away, he does it again.

The children come up with their nurse, and Edna wants to talk to them but they are interested only in the bonbons. The sun is setting, and Adele gathers up her sewing to leave. She complains of faintness, and Edna and Robert rush to help her. Afterwards Edna wonders if Adele had been faking.

Edna watches Adele walk away and watches her children run and cling to her. She picks up the little one despite her doctor's orders not to lift anything.

After Adele leaves, Robert asks Edna if she is going bathing. Edna says no, but Robert insists and they walk away together to the beach.

Chapter VI is only one page, and is a break from the plot. First Edna wonders why she first said no, and then so easily yes, to going to the beach with Robert. She is beginning to sense something in herself, but at this point it only confuses her and causes her anguish.

The narrator tells us that Edna is beginning to recognize her place in the world, and hints that most women never see this. And like all such beginnings, it is chaotic and dangerous.

Finally, the sea is described as seductive and sensuous, with a voice that speaks to the soul.

Analysis

In Chapter V, we see further the intimacy between Robert and Edna and learn that Robert devotes himself each summer to one woman. It is obviously understood at Grand Isle that Robert is not to be taken seriously. However, Edna, as we already know, is not familiar with Creole customs and can't help but take him seriously. She finds it offensive when he rests his head on her arm, yet he clearly thinks nothing of it.

We are introduced to Edna's love of beauty and art. Her love of beauty is shown through Adele, whom Edna likes to gaze at "as she might look upon a faultless Madonna." Her love of art is shown through her sketching. She "felt in it a satisfaction of a kind which no other employment afforded her." Yet she is very critical of herself as an artist; she crumples up a sketch of Adele because it doesn't look like her, even though it is a "fair enough piece of work."

We also see that she does in fact love her children, although she does not always feel motherly. When they come to the house looking for candy, "she sought to detain them for a little talk and some pleasantry." It sounds as though she were talking about adults rather than children. In fact, the children have no wish to stay. In contrast, Adele's children flutter around her skirts, and she picks the youngest one up despite her doctor's orders not to lift anything.

Again the sea comes into play, this time with a new adjective attached to it. The breeze that comes up is "charged with the seductive odor of the sea." Later after Robert invites her for a swim, the sea has a "sonorous murmur," which reached her like a "loving but imperative entreaty." The sea is becoming seductive; its pull on her is getting stronger.

Chapter VI is really an interlude in the narrative. Chopin is letting us know that the awakening is beginning; Edna is beginning to see her place in the world and to want more. Chopin is also telling us that such an awakening can be dangerous, even life-threatening. Finally, Chopin is using foreshadowing, telling us that the touch of the sea is an embrace Edna may not want to leave.

Study Questions

1. What is clear about Edna and Robert's relationship?

  2. Why is Robert allowed to spend so much time with married women at Grand Isle?

  3. How does Edna feel about Adele's beauty?

  4. Why does Edna sketch?

  5. Why does Edna repulse Robert's head from her arm?

  6. Why does Edna crumple up the picture of Adele?

  7. How is the sea described here?

  8. Why did Edna go bathing with Robert?

  9. What is Edna beginning to realize?

  10. Why is Edna's realization potentially dangerous?

Answers

  1. It is clear that they are very intimate.

  2. He is considered safe because nobody ever takes him seriously.

  3. She loves to gaze at Adele and wishes to sketch her.

  4. Sketching gives her satisfaction that no other work does.

  5. She does not think it is proper for Robert to touch her like that.

  6. The picture does not look like Adele.

  7. The sea is seductive, sensuous, embracing—like a lover.

  8. She was following an impulse that she didn't understand.

  9. Edna is beginning to realize her position in the universe and her relation to the rest of the world.

  10. It is a beginning, and all beginnings are chaotic and disturbing. Additionally, women are not usually graced with such realizations so there will clearly be consequences.

Suggested Essay Topics

  1. Describe the changes Edna has gone through so far.

  2. How does the sea fit in with Edna's awakening?

Chapter VII

New Characters:

The Lovers: *a young, unmarried couple who are oblivious to all but themselves*

Summary

Edna, usually a woman of outward reserve, is beginning to loosen up a bit at Grand Isle, mostly under the influence of Adele's beauty and candor.

One morning the women go together to the beach, and although the children are left behind, Adele brings her needlework. Both women are described as tall, with Adele having a feminine and matronly figure, while Edna's is "long, clean and symmetrical." Similarly Adele is dressed in white ruffles while Edna is wearing white and brown linen.

At the beach, the Pontelliers and Ratignolles share adjoining compartments, and Edna pulls a rug and pillows out so the women can sit down in the shade against the front of the building. There are few people about; they see the lovers, the lady in black, and a few others further away.

Edna is gazing at the sea in such an absorbed way that Adele asks her what she is thinking. Edna begins to talk of her childhood in Kentucky and a particular day when she walked aimlessly through a green meadow. She says she feels the same way sometimes at Grand Isle. Adele takes her hand and begins caressing it, which is difficult at first for Edna who is not used to expressions of affection.

Next Edna begins thinking and talking about past affections she had for certain young men; she had been very passionate about them. In contrast her marriage to Leonce was "purely an accident," one that closed forever the world of romance for her, although she had grown fond of him. Her feelings for her children were inconsistent; she felt free of unwanted responsibility when they were not around.

Just after these "confessions," Robert approaches with several children. The women get up; Edna joins the children, and Robert walks Adele back up to her cottage.

Analysis

Here we see that Edna has always been "different" and that she perceived early the difference between "the outward existence which conforms, the inward life which questions."

Again we see the physical descriptions of Edna and Adele relating to their personalities. Edna's figure is noble and symmetrical while Adele's (from Chapter IV) is plump and matronly. Here Edna is wearing a cool muslin dress with a streak of brown running through it. Adele is dressed in pure white, in a fluffy dress with ruffles. Edna's physical being is always described in more masculine terms than Adele's.

Sitting at the beach, Edna, as always, is focused on the sea. She is gazing so intently that Adele asks what she is thinking about. Edna, who is usually very reserved, is drawn into unusual candor by Adele's beauty and charm. She tells Adele a story about her childhood in Kentucky, walking aimlessly through a green meadow, and adds that she feels that way now sometimes—aimless and unguided. Her awakening is still new to her, and it feels strange. She's heading into uncharted waters and therefore has no guidance.

When Adele takes Edna's hand, Edna is shocked at first, not being used to expressions of affection. This is part of her repression, something she longs to break free of. She tells Adele of old passions, of her infatuation with romance. She also tells how she gave it up when she married Leonce. For Edna romance and marriage are mutually exclusive.

Edna also tells Adele something about her feelings for her children. Edna loves her children but feels weighed down with a responsibility that is suited to her nature. She feels relief when they are away.

Sharing with Adele is like "the first breath of freedom" for Edna. She feels "intoxicated." It is the first letting go of the repression she grew up with.

Study Questions

1. What is Edna's attitude toward sharing confidences?

2. What is it about Adele that started to bring Edna out of her shell?

3. Why does Adele insist on bringing her needlework to the beach?

4. What is the difference in the way Edna and Adele dressed for the beach?

5. What is Edna gazing at when Adele begins questioning her thoughts?

6. What does Edna's childhood meadow story tell her and us about her present state?

7. Why is Edna confused when Adele begins stroking her hand?

8. What is different about Edna's relationship with Leonce and the other men she talks about?

9. How does Edna feel when she is away from her children?

10. How does Edna feel after sharing about herself with Adele?

Answers

1. She is not used to sharing confidences; she had always understood that she had a secret inner life.

2. Edna is drawn out first by Adele's beauty and then by her complete candor.

3. As a mother-woman, Adele cannot be without some reminder of that role.

4. Edna wears a cool white and brown muslin dress that has a fairly severe line. Adele wears a pure white, frilly, ruffled dress. Edna's dress has a more masculine tone, Adele's a more feminine.

5. She is gazing at the sea.

6. It tells us that she currently feels aimless and unguided, just as she did then.

7. Edna is not used to any displays of affection.

8. She married Leonce for practical reasons, with no feelings of passion or love. The other men she had been infatuated with, feeling tremendous passion.

9. She feels as if she is free of a responsibility that she is not suited for.

10. She feels intoxicated, as if she has just had her first taste of freedom.

Suggested Essay Topics

1. Compare Edna's feelings for Leonce with her feelings for the soldier, the tragedian, and Robert.

2. Why does Edna's sharing feel like freedom?

Chapter VIII

New Character:

Victor Lebrun: *the younger brother of Robert*

Summary

As soon as Robert and Adele begin their walk away from the beach, Adele asks Robert to leave Edna alone. She is afraid that Edna might take him seriously. In his defense, Robert tells a story about Alcee Arobin and the consul's wife and several other sordid stories. Then he declares that Edna would never take him seriously. He makes Adele a cup of bouillon and leaves for the main house.

On his way, he passes the lovers, who are oblivious to everything around them. He looks for Edna and the children, but not seeing them, he goes to his mother's house. She is busy at her sewing machine.

Robert and his mother engage in some conversation and then they call out to Victor, who is driving off somewhere. He refuses to answer, however, and Madame Lebrun becomes very annoyed with the willful Victor. Madame Lebrun speculates that all would be well if only her husband had not died so young.

Madame Lebrun then tells Robert that a suitor of hers would be going to Mexico and has invited Robert to join him.

Analysis

Adele, sensing Edna's romantic inclinations, warns Robert to stay away from her. She reminds him that Edna is not a Creole and might take him seriously. Robert is offended but understands that he would not be able to keep company with the ladies the way he does if anybody took him seriously. He then tells a story about Alcee Arobin having an affair with somebody's wife. He is trying to differentiate himself from Alcee who obviously does not live by the same rules.

When Robert leaves Adele's cottage, he sees the lovers, who as usual are oblivious to all but themselves. The lovers symbolize premarriage romance—everything that Edna wants and does not have with Leonce.

Finally we learn that Robert has been invited to Mexico. Although we already know that he has been talking about going for years, this invitation lets us know that he might finally be going.

Study Questions

1. What is different about Adele's eyes when she talks to Robert?
2. What is Adele's fear when she asks Robert to leave Edna alone?
3. How does Adele explain that fear to Robert?
4. Why is it important that nobody take Robert seriously?
5. What does Robert tell Adele about Alcee Arobin?
6. What is Robert's thought about Edna?
7. How do the lovers walk?
8. Why does Madame Lebrun have someone else working the treadle of her sewing machine?
9. How does Madame Lebrun account for things going wrong in her life and the world?
10. What news does Madame Lebrun have for Robert?

Answers

1. They are filled with thoughtfulness and speculation.
2. She is afraid that Edna will take Robert's attentions seriously.

3. She is afraid because Edna is not a Creole.

4. If Robert's attentions to married women were taken seriously, he would be thought a scoundrel and no proper women would associate with him.

5. Robert tells Adele about Alcee's affair with the consul's wife.

6. He believes she would never take him seriously.

7. The lovers walk as if there were no ground beneath their feet.

8. Creole women don't do anything that might imperil their health.

9. She blames it on the fact that her husband died so early in their marriage.

10. A friend of hers is going to Vera Cruz and Robert has been invited to join him.

Suggested Essay Topics

1. What has Edna said or done that would make Adele worry that she might take Robert's affections seriously?

2. How does not being a Creole affect Edna? Why is it difficult for outsiders in any society to adjust and fit in?

Chapter IX

New Character:

Mademoiselle Reisz: *a loner at Grand Isle; a gifted pianist who becomes very close to Edna*

Summary

It is now Saturday night, a few weeks after the conversation between Robert and Adele. The main house is all lit up and decorated, and all the guests are there for relaxation and entertainment. Even the children are permitted to stay up later than usual, until after ice cream and cake are served. The Farival twins perform the same songs as always on the piano, a little girl performs a dance,

and a brother and sister give recitations. Then everyone dances while Adele plays the piano.

While Adele is playing, Edna conjures up an image of a naked man standing alone and hopeless on the beach, watching a bird fall from the sky.

Robert leaves to get Mademoiselle Reisz, who agrees, to everyone's happiness, to play the piano. Edna is very fond of music; if it is well played, it evokes pictures in her mind. This time, however, she sees no pictures. Instead, the music invokes great passion, and she finds herself shaking and crying. Mademoiselle Reisz finishes playing and leaves, happy with Edna's response.

The party breaks up shortly after Mademoiselle Reisz leaves, although many of the guests decide to go bathing at Robert's suggestion.

Analysis

The chapter opens with entertainment being provided for the guests, by the guests. The Farival twins repeat their earlier performance, reminding us again of Zampa's romantic death at sea.

Adele plays piano while everyone dances. She plays only because it was a "means of brightening the home and making it attractive." Everything Adele does is for others. She is in direct contrast to Mademoiselle Reisz who is a true artist but has no family or love in her life. These are the two extremes surrounding Edna. Mademoiselle Reisz, physically, is the extreme opposite of Adele. She is short, thin and ugly, and nobody really likes her. This is what happens to women who forsake marriage and motherhood.

Adele plays a piece that Edna names "Solitude." While listening, Edna finds herself conjuring up an image of a solitary naked man by the seashore. His attitude was one of "hopeless resignation" as he watches a bird in flight. This is how Edna feels: alone, lonely, unable to fly away and be free. It can also be seen as foreshadowing of Edna's fate. The same image comes up in Chapter XXXIX, only it has a slightly different feel to it there.

When Mademoiselle Reisz plays the piano, Edna is stirred by a whole new set of emotions, notably passion. She is so moved she sobs. Edna has never felt that sort of passion before but will now long to feel it again.

Study Questions

1. Why is the hall lit up and decorated?

2. Why are the Pontellier children exerting authority over the other children?

3. What songs do the Farival twins play?

4. Why does Adele keep up with her music?

5. What is Edna looking at when she sat on the windowsill?

6. What does Mademoiselle Reisz look like?

7. What does Edna think of when she hears the song Adele plays that she calls "Solitude"?

8. What is different about Edna as she hears Mademoiselle Reisz's first chords on the piano?

9. What is Edna's reaction to Mademoiselle Reisz's music?

10. Why does Mademoiselle Reisz think Edna is the only one worth playing for?

Answers

1. It is Saturday night, and all the guests are gathered for an evening of entertainment.

2. Leonce had brought them colored sheets of the comic papers, and all the children want to see them.

3. They play the duet from *Zampa* and the overture from *The Poet and the Peasant.*

4. She and her husband considered it a means of brightening their home and making it attractive.

5. She is looking at the moon casting its light across the restless sea.

6. She is small and ugly, with a weazened face and body.

7. She thinks of a naked, lonely man standing on the seashore, looking at a distant bird with hopeless resignation.

8. It is the first time she is truly ready to hear an artist and for Edna, this means to hear the truth.

9. She feels stirred by passion, as if waves are beating against her body.

10. She thinks Edna is the only one who is visibly and genuinely moved.

Suggested Essay Topics

1. What is the difference between the way Adele and Mademoiselle Reisz play the piano? How does each one's style affect Edna?

2. What is the similarity between Edna and the image of the lonely man she conjures up while listening to Adele play?

Chapter X

Summary

The guests walk in little groups down to the beach, but Robert lingers behind with the lovers. Edna wonders why he is not coming; she misses him when he is not around her. The sea is quiet and the moon is bright.

Edna had been trying all summer to learn to swim, but tonight she finally is able to swim. She is so happy she shouts for joy and swims out by herself as far as she can go. While out there, she feels a momentary twinge of panic, but manages to swim safely back in. After that she changes into dry clothes and leaves, despite protestations from the other guests.

Robert overtakes her as she is walking home, and they chat about spirits and the dreamlike quality of the night. At one point Edna becomes offended, thinking Robert is mocking her feelings. When they reach her cottage, Edna stretches out in the hammock to wait for Leonce. Robert waits until he thinks she is asleep and then leaves. She watches him walk away.

Analysis

Edna is beginning to realize how much she misses Robert when he is not around. The imagery continues to get more romantic, erotic, and poetic as her feelings get stronger. At the beach she smells "a

tangle of the sea smell and of weeds and damp, new-plowed earth, mingled with the heavy perfume of a field of white blossoms."

Edna swims for the first time tonight and revels in the power she suddenly has over her body and soul. This is another awakening. She wants to swim far out, "where no woman had ever swum before." She feels intoxicated, as she did in Chapter VII when she opened up to Adele. This feeling of intoxication is repeated throughout the novel, whenever Edna feels a surge of personal power. It is contrasted with the numerous periods of languor or stupor, which come over her when she feels powerless or hopeless.

Edna feels a moment of panic and sees a quick vision of death when she sees how far out she has swum, but she rallies her strength and swims back. She is still unsure of and frightened by her new sense of freedom and power, despite the joy she feels.

The story about spirits that Robert tells Edna as he walks her home is important because, although he does not know it, a new spirit has truly entered into Edna; she has had her first real taste of freedom. This sense of magic also sets the stage for Edna's "first-felt throbbings of desire" for Robert.

Study Questions

1. How does Edna feel when Robert is not around?

2. What is the odor Edna smells down by the sea?

3. Why had Edna not been able to learn to swim?

4. What is different about this night?

5. How does Edna feel when she starts swimming?

6. What is she looking for when she swims out?

7. What does Edna experience after she swims a certain distance?

8. How does Edna describe the night to Robert when he walks her home?

9. How does Robert describe it?

10. What happens in the silence when Edna is in the hammock and Robert is sitting by her?

Answers

1. She misses him and wonders why he is not with her.

2. She smells a tangle of the sea, weeds, damp, new-plowed earth and the heavy perfume of a field of white blossoms.

3. She feels an ungovernable dread in the water unless someone is nearby.

4. Edna is realizing her power.

5. She feels exulted, as if she had been given power finally over her body and soul. She wants to swim far out, where no woman has swum before.

6. She is looking for space and solitude, reaching out for the unlimited in which to lose herself.

7. She has a quick vision of death that makes her temporarily weak.

8. She feels as if it is a dream.

9. Robert tells Edna that there is a spirit out, who searches for someone worthy to inhabit and that tonight the spirit found Edna.

10. They feel the throbbings of desire for one another.

Suggested Essay Topics

1. How does learning to swim contribute to Edna's awakening?

2. What is the significance of Robert's story about the spirit that haunts the shores and his statement to Edna that tonight the spirit found her?

Chapter XI

Summary

When Leonce returns to the cottage, he finds Edna lying in the hammock and asks, then demands, that she come inside. Edna refuses, realizing that this is the first time she has ever done so.

Leonce had prepared for bed already, but he goes outside and sits in the rocker with a glass of wine and a cigar. After a while, Edna feels her will leaving her; she begins to feel helpless again. She arises and goes inside and asks Leonce if he is joining her. He tells her he will come in after he finishes his cigar.

Analysis

Edna's refusal to go inside at Leonce's command marks her first rebellion, powered by her swim and the spirits of the night. She realized that her will had "blazed up," and that she could have not done other than refuse him. Her "awakening" is powerful and has more control of her than she has of it at times.

Unfortunately, Leonce still wins this first round. As he sits smoking on the porch, Edna again begins to feel "the realities pressing against her soul." This is the reality of convention that Edna is fighting against, the convention that gives the husband control over the wife. Her feeling of exuberance turns to one of helplessness and weakness, and she has to yield.

Study Questions

1. Where does Leonce find Edna when he returns to the cottage?
2. What does Leonce say to her?
3. What would Edna normally have done in this situation?
4. What is different about this night?
5. How does Leonce respond to Edna's refusal to obey him?
6. How long is Leonce preparing to stay outside.
7. How does Edna feel when she realizes Leonce is staying outside with her?
8. Why does Edna go back inside?

9. What does Leonce do after Edna goes inside?

10. Who is the winner in this battle between Edna and Leonce?

Answers

1. She is lying in the hammock on the front porch.

2. He demands that she come inside.

3. She would have given in to Leonce out of habit.

4. Edna's will had blazed up, stubborn and resistant.

5. He put something on over his pajamas and went outside with a cigar and a glass of wine.

6. He is prepared to stay outside as long as Edna does.

7. She feels like she had awakened from a delicious dream to the ugly realities of her life.

8. The exultation she felt is gone, and she feels helpless and tired.

9. He stays outside to finish his cigar.

10. Leonce wins because Edna feels forced by her crushed spirit to finally go inside.

Suggested Essay Topics

1. What are the realities that Edna is talking about when she says she feels again "the realities pressing into her soul"? Why do these realities cause her to go inside?

2. Put yourself in Leonce's place. Describe your reaction to Edna's refusal to come inside.

Chapter XII

New Characters:

Mariequita: *a "mischievous," carefree Spanish girl who works at Grand Isle*

Baudelet: *an old sailor who takes people by boat to Mass at Cheniere Caminada*

Summary

Edna sleeps badly and is up and dressed early. Only a few others are up, those who intend to go to mass at the Cheniere. Edna sends Madame Lebrun's servant to wake up Robert, to tell him to come to mass with her. They each have coffee and a roll, and then join the others at the wharf. The lovers are there, the lady in black, old Monsieur Farival, and a young girl named Mariequita whom Robert knows and speaks to in Spanish.

Edna stares at Mariequita, and Mariequita asks Robert if Edna is Robert's lover. Robert answers that she is married.

Edna feels light and free again sailing on the bay, and Robert asks her to go with him to Grand Terre the following day. They chat about it for a while in an intimate manner, and then everybody goes to the church except Baudelet and Mariequita.

Analysis

Here Chopin shows us how Edna's "awakening" has taken hold of her; she is not acting with purpose so much as "blindly following whatever impulse moved her." Edna has moved forward from feeling "aimless" and "unguided" in Chapter VII to feeling as if "alien hands" were directing her. She asks Robert to join her for mass without thinking about it, without even noticing that she had never done that before.

Mariequita, who is very open, points out the truth and the irony about Edna and Robert's relationship, although nobody realizes it. When she asks Robert if Edna is his lover, and Robert answers that she is married, Mariequita responds with a story about a man who ran away on a boat with a married lady. Obviously, Edna's marriage is not going to protect them from their feelings. In fact, Edna and

Robert are on a boat together as the story is being told, and they make plans to go sailing together again the following day. Mariequita and Robert also share a laugh about the lovers not being married; obviously it is not just Edna for whom marriage and romance are separate.

Study Questions

1. How does Edna sleep after finally going inside?
2. What is the something Edna feels is unattainable?
3. Was it usual for Edna to invite Robert to mass?
4. What does Robert note about Edna when they are drinking their coffee?
5. What does Mariequita look like?
6. What does Mariequita ask Robert?
7. Does Robert deny it?
8. What does Mariequita think of the fact that Edna is married?
9. Why is it understood that the lovers aren't married?
10. What do Robert and Edna talk about on the boat?

Answers

1. She sleeps badly, disturbed by dreams that leave her with a sense of something unattainable.
2. She feels that her freedom is unattainable.
3. No. She had never done it before, although neither one of them realize how unusual it was.
4. He says that she often lacks forethought.
5. She has a round face and pretty black eyes, but her feet are broad and coarse.
6. She asks if he and Edna are lovers.
7. No. He only answers that Edna is married and has children.
8. Mariequita knows that fact would not stop two lovers from

being together and tells a story to Robert about a man and a married woman who ran off together in a boat.

9. People think that marriage and romance don't go together.

10. They plan some trips together alone on the boat.

Suggested Essay Topics

1. What other examples do we see of Edna's lack of forethought?

2. How does Edna feel about marriage and romance and why?

Chapter XIII

New Characters:

Madame Antoine: *a village woman at Cheniere Caminada whose house Edna stays in when she feels ill*

Tonie: *the son of Madame Antoine*

Summary

Edna begins to feel tired and sick during the service and leaves before it is over. Robert follows her outside and suggests they go to Madame Antoine's. Madame Antoine welcomes them in and brings Edna to a room with a large, white four-posted bed. Robert sits outside with Madame Antoine to wait for Tonie. Edna bathes in the basin, undresses, and luxuriates in the smell of the bed and the feel of her body. Eventually she falls asleep.

When Edna awakes, she feels as if she has been asleep a long time. She washes again and walks into the adjoining room where she enjoys the food and drink Madame Antoine has set out for her. When she finds Robert, they joke that she slept for 100 years, and they are the only two people left.

Robert prepares more food, and they eat a hearty meal, deciding that since the others have already returned to Grand Isle they will wait till the sun goes down to return. Madame Antoine returns and tells them stories under the night moon. Then they leave in Tonie's boat.

Analysis

We see for sure here that Edna's awakening is not religious in nature; in fact her strict religious upbringing was one of the causes of her repression. Now free to come or go, she gets sick while in church and has to leave. This sickness also gives her more time to be alone with Robert. Away from the stodgy church, Edna can again hear the voice of the sea and continue with her romantic getaway.

Alone and partially undressed in Madame Antoine's bed, Edna experiences an erotic enjoyment of her own body. This growing sexuality is part of her awakening.

When Edna wakes up, she and Robert continue the fairy tale fantasy they have been sharing. Edna asks Robert how many years she has been asleep, and he answers, "one hundred." He then tells her that he has been guarding her slumber since they are the only people left on earth. Later when the sun goes down, Edna can hear "the whispering voices of dead men and the click of muffled gold." When she and Robert finally leave in Tonie's boat, "misty spirit forms were prowling in the shadows."

Edna eats when she first wakes up, and she eats again with Robert. Her appetite, her pleasure in food and drink, is part of the sensuousness that is beginning to surround her.

Study Questions

1. What happens to Edna during the mass?
2. What is the only sound Edna hears after she leaves the mass?
3. Where does Robert take Edna to rest?
4. What does Edna do when she is alone in the bedroom?
5. How does Edna feel laying in the bed?
6. How does Edna feel when she awakes?
7. How does Edna turn their trip into a romantic fairy tale?
8. What is Robert's response?
9. What does Robert do for Edna after she awakes?
10. How is the fairy tale quality continued when Robert and Edna leave?

Answers

1. She is overcome with a feeling of oppression and drowsiness, and her head begins to ache.

2. She hears the voice of the sea whispering through the reeds.

3. He takes her to Madame Antoine's house at the far end of the village.

4. After she bathes her face, neck, and arms, she takes off her shoes and stockings and stretches herself out on the bed.

5. She feels luxurious and sensuous, enjoying the way her body feels in the bed.

6. As if she had been asleep a very long time. Additionally, she is very hungry.

7. She asks Robert how many years she has been asleep and if they are the only two people left on earth.

8. Robert plays along, saying she was asleep for 100 years, and he had been guarding her sleep.

9. He cooks a meal for her.

10. They are alone together in the boat in the dark, with spirit forms lurking in the shadows and phantom ships upon the water.

Suggested Essay Topics

1. How does the idea of fairy tale fit in with Edna's awakening and her relationship with Robert?

2. What is Edna's attitude about food and eating? What does this tell us about her personality?

Chapter XIV

Summary

When Edna returns to her cottage at nine o'clock, Adele, who has been watching the children, tells Edna that Etienne, the younger of Edna's sons, would not go to sleep. Edna sits in the rocker with him and soothes him to sleep. Leonce, after being dissuaded from fetching Edna back earlier, has gone to Klein's.

Robert leaves and goes for a solitary walk after Edna points out that they have been together the whole day. Edna, too, stays alone, in the cottage, rather than join the others. She realizes that she has changed since last summer and that in fact she is different than she has ever been before.

She wonders why Robert has not stayed, and wishes that he had. She begins singing a song that he had sung to her on the boat.

Analysis

Edna is very loving and attentive to her children when she returns from Cheniere Caminada because she is feeling good about herself. This is part of her central conflict. She can love them when she's not feeling repressed by them.

Leonce, as usual, is not around. His role as husband is merely that of provider. He feels no responsibility to help around the house or spend time with his wife.

While Edna is awaiting Leonce's return, she realizes that she is beginning to change; she just doesn't understand the significance of the change yet. Although she is waiting for Leonce, she spends the time thinking about Robert.

Study Questions

1. Why is Etienne still up when Edna returns?
2. How does Edna act with Etienne when she returns home?
3. Why is Edna so loving toward Etienne at this time?
4. Why is Adele staying with the children?
5. Why does Adele leave immediately after Edna returned?
6. How does Robert show his feelings as he says goodnight to Edna?

7. What does Robert do after he left Edna?

8. What does Edna realize about this summer at Grand Isle?

9. How does Edna feel about Robert's leaving?

10. What does Edna do while waiting for Leonce to return?

Answers

1. He had refused to go to bed and had made a scene.

2. She coddles and caresses him and is very loving and tender.

3. She is feeling good about herself.

4. Leonce left to go to Klein's for the evening.

5. Monsieur Ratignolle hates to be alone.

6. He presses her hand.

7. He goes for a solitary walk by the sea.

8. She realizes that she is somehow different than she had been in previous years.

9. She regrets that he left; it has become natural to have him around.

10. She sings the song that Robert sang to her on the boat.

Suggested Essay Topics

1. Describe Edna's relationship with her children and why it changes based on her feelings about herself.

2. What are some of the ways Edna has changed already?

Chapter XV

Summary

A few days later, Edna enters the dining room a little late and learns from several people at once that Robert is going away to Mexico, and he is leaving for New Orleans that very evening. This comes as a surprise to her, and she shows it. Robert looks embarrassed and uneasy. He explains to everyone at the table, in a defensive voice, that he is going to meet someone in Vera Cruz and that he just decided that afternoon to go.

The lovers, as usual, speak only to each other. Everyone else is buzzing about the trip. Adele warns him about the Mexicans, whom she does not trust. Edna asks him what time he is leaving and then leaves the room.

She goes back to her cottage where she busies herself with little things and then tells the children a story. The little black girl comes by to invite Edna to Madame Lebrun's to sit until Robert leaves, but Edna feigns illness. Adele stops by and Edna expresses her shock, with which Adele agrees. Then Adele leaves to join the group.

Robert finally stops by, and Edna berates him for not telling her of his plan. She tells him how she looks forward to seeing him and spending time together. Robert agrees and intimates that this is the reason he is leaving. He holds out his hand, and Edna clings to it, entreating him to write to her. Robert agrees and leaves rather stiffly. Edna tries to hold back her tears and her feelings, but she is forced to recognize her feelings of infatuation.

Analysis

Robert's announcement that he is leaving for Mexico takes Edna completely by surprise. Because she feels controlled by outside forces to some extent, she never thinks about the future. Additionally she is very self-absorbed. It does not occur to her that Robert might have plans of his own that don't include her.

We see another side of Adele here. She is a beautiful mother-woman, but she is also a bigot and clearly not very intelligent. It is clear that her opinions come from somewhere outside her. This is just one of the characteristics of the mother-woman.

Edna refuses to go to the Lebruns because she is hurt and angry. She is experiencing a childish temper tantrum. Robert makes it clear that he is leaving because of what is happening between him and Edna. He is a man of honor, and if he cannot have her, then he wants to leave. Edna has no concept of what he is feeling. She cannot see past her own feelings, which she finally recognizes as infatuation of the type she used to feel before she married Leonce.

Study Questions

1. How does Edna learn that Robert is going to Mexico?
2. What does Edna do with her feeling of bewilderment?
3. How does Robert look when he sees Edna's face?
4. How does Robert explain his sudden departure?
5. How does this news affect Edna's appetite?
6. What does Adele warn Robert about?
7. What does Edna do when she goes back to her room?
8. Why does Edna refuse to go to the Lebruns?
9. What does Robert make clear to Edna before he leaves?
10. What does Edna realize after Robert leaves?

Answers

1. Several people tell her at once when she enters the dining room late for dinner one afternoon.
2. She lets it show on her face.
3. He looks embarrassed and uneasy.
4. He was meeting his mother's friend in Vera Cruz, and he needed to get to New Orleans to pack in time to make the ship that would take him there by the appointed day.
5. She forces herself to finish her soup but can't eat her stew.
6. She tells him that Mexicans are not to be trusted.
7. She busies herself with little odds and ends and helps put the boys to bed.
8. She claims she is tired, but the truth is she can't bear to watch Robert go.
9. He is leaving because of his strong feelings for Edna.
10. She realizes that she loves him.

Suggested Essay Topics
1. Why does Robert feel the need to leave?

2. How does Edna's realization of her love for Robert contribute to her awakening?

Chapter XVI

Summary

Mademoiselle Reisz asks Edna if she misses Robert. In fact she misses him greatly and feels that her life has been dulled. She talks about him constantly and looks at old family pictures with Madame Lebrun. She wishes there were a recent picture for her to look at. Madame Lebrun shows her a letter Robert had written, and Edna feels jealous that he wrote to his mother rather than her.

Even Leonce assumes that Edna misses Robert. Leonce saw Robert in the city before he left for Mexico, and Edna pesters him with questions. She does not find it at all "grotesque" that she is making so much of his absence; in fact, she does not think much about it at all and does not feel the need to voice her feelings.

Edna prefers to keep her thoughts and emotions to herself. She once told Adele that she would never sacrifice herself for her children, although she would give up her life. The two women argued about it, and Edna felt like they were speaking two different languages; Adele did not understand.

Nonetheless Edna answers Mademoiselle Reisz's question honestly, if lightly. Then they chat about the Lebruns, and Mademoiselle Reisz has nasty things to say about both Madame Lebrun and Victor. Edna feels depressed by Mademoiselle Reisz's venom and leaves her to go bathing, although she had not planned to. She swims for a long time, feeling thrilled and invigorated. She hopes that Mademoiselle Reisz won't wait for her, but she does. Mademoiselle Reisz gives Edna her city address and invites her to come visit as the summer is nearly over, and they will both be leaving Grand Isle within the next two weeks.

Analysis

Edna says that swimming is the only pleasure she has. This is because when she is swimming she feels powerful, like she is in control of her body and soul. The rest of the time she feels the reality of her constraint and the reality of Robert's absence. Swimming is also a sensuous experience for Edna, as she feels a longing for Robert.

Edna feels jealous that Robert wrote to his mother rather than her. This shows the immaturity and the intensity of her feelings. The fact that everybody assumes she misses him shows how nobody, including Leonce, takes the relationship seriously—nobody but Robert and Edna, and Edna doesn't even realize how seriously she takes it.

Adele does not understand Edna's statement that she would die for her children but would never sacrifice herself, which brings back a theme from the parrot in the first chapter. As long as Edna mimics everyone else, she can get along and be understood. As soon as she starts becoming her own person, she is suddenly speaking a different language that only she understands. Thus, it is clear right here that Edna cannot have her awakening and continue to live in her old world.

Edna gets depressed by Mademoiselle Reisz's mean talk, but she is drawn to her nonetheless, because she is an artist and stirs the passion in Edna that Edna longs to feel.

Study Questions

1. What does Edna consider to be the only pleasurable moments she has?

2. How does Edna keep close to Robert after he leaves?

3. How does Leonce feel about Edna's missing Robert?

4. Why is Edna jealous when she read's Robert's letter?

5. What does Edna tell Adele about her children?

6. Why can't Adele understand what Edna is talking about?

7. What does Edna mean when she says she wouldn't sacrifice herself for her children?

8.   What do Edna and Mademoiselle Reisz talk about as they walk to the beach?

9.   Why does Edna spend time with Mademoiselle Reisz if the woman's meanness depresses her?

10. How does Edna swim now?

Answers

1.   She feels pleasure only when she is swimming.

2.   She keeps close to him by talking about him to everyone who knows him and by looking at Madame Lebrun's family photographs.

3.   He doesn't give it a second thought; it would never occur to a Creole man that his wife could be unfaithful.

4.   He wrote to his mother and not to her.

5.   She said that she would die for her children, but she would not sacrifice herself.

6.   Edna is becoming her own person and speaking a new language.

7.   She won't let her life be controlled by her responsibility to her children. She needs to be her own person, apart from her role as mother.

8.   They talk about the Lebrun family and how Robert and Victor had a big fight the previous year over Mariequita.

9.   She needs to be with an artist, someone who can inspire passion.

10. She swims with an abandon that thrills and invigorates her.

Suggested Essay Topics

1.   Describe the gulf that has grown between Edna and Adele. Why doesn't Adele understand what Edna is telling her?

2.   What is considered essential by Edna compared to what would be considered essential by other women of her time?

Chapter XVII

Summary

The story has now moved to New Orleans. There is a description of the Pontelliers' house on Esplanade Street, which is very beautiful and luxurious. Leonce is very fond of walking around the house and taking pleasure in his possessions.

Since her wedding six years earlier, Tuesday has been a reception day for Edna. There is a constant stream of female callers all afternoon, and sometimes at night the men would join their wives. One Tuesday night at dinner, several weeks after their return to the city, Leonce notices that Edna is not in her reception dress but is wearing an ordinary housedress. Edna tells him she went out for the day and thus was not home to receive the callers.

Leonce reprimands her, reminding her that they have to observe convention. Then he asks to see the cards that were left, so he would know who called. He begins to read the names aloud, commenting on each one as he reads. He is upset when one of the ladies' husbands is a wealthy man whom he is afraid to snub. Edna gets angry, and Leonce, saying the food is a disaster and claiming it is Edna's fault for not looking after the cook, leaves to eat at the club. Although this scene was not unfamiliar, Edna's reaction is. She sits and eats her dinner by herself and then goes up to her room, still not bothering with the cook.

When Edna gets to her room, she stands by the open window to look at the garden below, which seems full of mystery. She contemplates that she is seeking and finding herself but feels devoid of hope. This makes her angry. She tears up the handkerchief in her hands and then throws her wedding ring down and stomps on it. Then she shatters a glass vase, feeling the need to destroy something.

A maid, hearing the noise, comes in and Edna explains that the vase had fallen. The maid picks up Edna's ring and hands it to her. Edna slips it back on her finger.

Analysis

We see again Leonce's view of the world. It is based on finance and ownership. He likes to walk through his house examining his possessions, which he enjoys because they belong to him. Unfortunately, he includes Edna among his possessions.

Leonce cannot understand why Edna abandoned her Tuesday reception, but his concern is only economic. He is afraid Edna will snub someone who is important to him in the business world. He is not at all concerned with her personally.

After their little fight, Leonce leaves to have dinner at the club. It is his constant escape, and he goes there whenever things are not to his liking.

Edna responds differently to the fight than she used to. "Her eyes flamed with some inward fire," and she finished her dinner alone and didn't run to fix things with the cook. She is no longer running to please Leonce, no longer intimidated by his disapproval.

However the fight does leave her feeling hopeless, and this makes her angry. "She wanted to destroy something." What she really wanted to destroy was her marriage, and in yet another attempted rebellion, she throws off her wedding ring and tries to crush it. In the end, however, she is defeated because she puts the ring back on her finger.

Study Questions

1. How does Leonce feel about his house in New Orleans?

2. What do Tuesdays mean for Edna?

3. What is Leonce angry about on this particular Tuesday?

4. Why is it so important to Leonce that Edna be home for her receptions?

5. Who does Leonce blame for the poorly cooked meal?

6. How does Edna react to Leonce's reprimand and departure for the club?

7. What does Edna seek in the garden that night?

8. What does Edna find in the garden?

9. How does Edna act out her anger?

10. How do we know that this rebellion ends in defeat as her first one did?

Answers

1. He likes to walk around admiring his possessions.

2. Tuesday is her traditional reception day, where other society women call on her during the afternoon.

3. Edna went out instead of being home to receive her guests.

4. It is important because it is the proper thing to do, and it would look bad for him if Edna didn't go along; ultimately it might affect him financially.

5. He blames Edna for the poorly cooked meal. He feels it is her job to keep watch over the cook.

6. Instead of her usual reaction, Edna finishes her meal by herself and says nothing to the cook.

7. She is looking for herself and for signs of hope.

8. The voices she hears are mournful and devoid of hope.

9. She tears up a handkerchief, breaks a glass vase, and throws off her wedding ring and tries to crush it with her shoe.

10. She puts her wedding ring back on after the maid picks it up.

Suggested Essay Topics

1. What is the real cause of Edna's anger? Why does she put her wedding ring back on?

2. How does Chopin use natural imagery to help the reader understand Edna's moods?

Chapter XVIII

Summary

The next morning Leonce asks Edna to meet him in the city to go shopping; she does not want to go shopping. He notes that Edna is not looking well; she is pale and very quiet. Edna watches him leave and watches the children playing. She feels no interest in anything around her. In fact she feels the outside world, including her children, has suddenly become alien and antagonistic.

Although Edna criticizes most of her sketches, she gathers up some of them and leaves the house to go visit Adele. She is thinking about Robert, feeling an "incomprehensible longing."

The Ratignolles live not far from the Pontelliers, in spacious apartments over Monsieur Ratignolle's drugstore. Every two weeks the Ratignolles give a musical party, and they were very popular. Edna considers their lifestyle to be very French and very foreign.

Adele looks more beautiful than ever, and Edna hopes she might someday paint her. She shows Adele her sketches. She knows her opinions are valueless but wants to hear the encouragement. Adele, of course, praises them highly and even shows them off to her husband when he comes in for his midday lunch. Monsieur Ratignolle is a good man, and he and Adele have a close relationship where they understand each other perfectly. When he speaks, Adele listens attentively, even laying down her fork so as to listen better.

Edna feels a little depressed after leaving them, finding nothing worthwhile in their domestic harmony. She feels some pity for Adele, who would never know a moment of anguish, never have a taste of "life's delirium."

Analysis

Edna, immersed in her defeat of the night before, feels hopeless and depressed. Her home does not interest her, and her children become antagonists who are trying to enslave her. They have become antagonists because if it were not for them, she could leave.

Edna tries to forget Robert, but she cannot. She is "under a spell," continuing the mystical and fairy tale terminology. Whenever she thinks of him, she feels an "incomprehensible" longing; it is incomprehensible to her because she has never felt anything like it before.

Edna has no confidence in herself as an artist; after all, wives and mothers cannot be artists. She goes to Adele's for encouragement and validation even though she knows Adele's opinion is worthless. Edna's awakening to beauty is shown here in her response to Adele, who looks "more beautiful than ever." She looks so beautiful that Edna wanted to paint her.

The narrator tells us that the Ratignolles understand each other perfectly and have fused into one being. This is supposed to be the goal of marriage. However, we know that the reason they have fused is because Adele has given up her identity. Even here she listens attentively to him, putting down her fork so as to listen better. We don't hear anything about him listening to her.

Witnessing this domestic bliss leaves Edna depressed and sad for Adele. Adele will never know the highs and lows of life, which Edna believes are signs that one is truly alive. Although she says she is not sure what she means by "life's delirium," it seems to be the fusion of true love with sexual passion. Adele's life is one of "blind contentment," not passion.

Study Questions

1. How does Edna feel about her children the morning after her fight with Leonce?

2. Why does Edna always find fault with her sketches?

3. Why does Edna take her sketches to Adele's?

4. What is Edna thinking about as she walks to Adele's?

5. What is symbolic about Edna considering the Ratignolles' life French and foreign?

6. What are Edna's first thoughts about Adele when she sees her?

7. What is one example given of the "fusion" the Ratignolles have accomplished in their marriage?

8. Why does Edna pity Adele after witnessing this marital bliss?

9. What does Edna mean by "life's delirium"?

10. Why is it important for Edna to feel both anguish and passion?

Answers

1. She considers her children part of "an alien world that has suddenly become antagonistic."

2. She has no confidence in herself as an artist.

3. She needs validation and encouragement.

4. She is thinking about Robert and how much she misses him.

5. The concept of their domestic bliss, of any marriage, has become foreign to her.

6. Edna thinks that Adele looks more beautiful than ever, and she would like to paint her picture.

7. Adele listens attentively to everything her husband says, even putting down her fork to listen better.

8. Edna pities Adele because Adele will never feel true anguish nor would she ever know "life's delirium."

9. Life's delirium is the combination of true love and sexual passion.

10. These feelings show her that she is truly alive, truly her own person.

Suggested Essay Topics

1. How is the Ratignolles' marriage different from the Pontelliers'?

2. What is it about Adele's and Edna's marriages that prevents them from knowing "life's delirium"? Why is Adele content with this while Edna is not?

Chapter XIX

Summary

Edna realizes that her outburst with the ring and vase had been childish and futile. Instead she begins to do and feel exactly as she pleases, including more painting. She completely abandons her Tuesday receptions and makes no efforts toward running the household. Leonce, who had always been courteous as long as Edna had been submissive, now grows angry at her insolence. He compares her to Adele, who keeps up with her music but also with all her responsibilities. Edna tells him to leave her alone, and he does. However he wonders if Edna is growing mentally unbalanced. He cannot see that she is actually becoming her true self.

Edna goes to her atelier at the top of the house to paint. She is working a lot, using everyone in the house as models. However none of her work satisfies her. Sometimes as she works she sings the song Robert had sung to her, and she would feel desire sweeping through her.

There are days when she is very happy, especially when she is alone and able to dream. There are also days when she is very unhappy and despairing, and she cannot work on those days.

Analysis

Edna realizes the futility of her temper tantrums and finds a better way to express her displeasure with Leonce and her desires for herself; she will simply abandon her pretense of being a good wife and do exactly as she pleases.

Leonce, as earlier described, was a good husband by societal standards. We find out here that he was courteous only because Edna was submissive. Now that she is defying him he becomes angry and rude. However, this only serves to strengthen Edna's resolve.

Leonce doesn't understand Edna's need to be alone in her atelier painting. He doesn't equate it with his constant need to escape to the club because only he is allowed to have such needs. He believes all of Edna's time should be spent on the advancement of her family's welfare. He wants her to be more like Adele, who plays music only for her family to enjoy, not out of any thought for her own pleasure.

Leonce thinks that Edna is not herself; he does not realize that she never had a self to be before. It is only now that she is developing a sense of self, and it is threatening to him. Chopin's language is a romantic image of rebirth. Edna is "daily casting aside that fictitious self which we assume like a garment with which to appear before the world." The "casting aside" brings to mind the shedding of old skin. Edna is crawling out of her cocoon and turning into a butterfly; Leonce wants to clip her wings.

Whenever Edna thinks of Robert, Chopin's language becomes romantic and sensual. Edna hears the "ripple of the water," sees the "glint of the moon on the bay," and feels the "soft gusty beating of the hot south wind."

Edna likes to be alone, where she can dream. It is important to her awakening that she is away from the realities of life enough to keep her hope alive.

Study Questions

1. Why is it more powerful for Edna to neglect her household than to have temper tantrums?
2. Why had Leonce always been a courteous husband?
3. How does Leonce's anger contribute to Edna's awakening?
4. How does Leonce feel about Edna's painting?
5. Why is Adele's piano playing different from Edna's painting?
6. What can't Leonce see about Edna when he says she's "not herself"?
7. Why does Edna notice the housemaid's back and shoulders?
8. How does Edna feels when she thinks of Robert?
9. When does Edna feel really happy?
10. What contributes to Edna's days of unhappiness?

Answers

1. Neglecting her household will get more of a reaction from Leonce than a temper tantrum and also gives her more of a sense of freedom.
2. Edna had always been submissive.
3. Leonce's anger makes her resolve never to take another step backward.
4. He thinks her time would be better spent working for the comfort of her family.
5. Adele plays piano for her family; Edna paints for herself.
6. He can't see that she had no self before; it is only now that she is actually becoming her true self.
7. She is becoming more of an artist and is noticing beauty more.
8. She feels filled with desire.

9.   She feels really happy when she is alone in the sun dreaming.

10.   She feels unhappy when feelings of hopelessness come over her, when she believes that her situation will never change.

Suggested Essay Topics

1.   Why is Edna's painting important to her awakening and her sense of independence?

2.   What does Edna mean when she says that Adele is not a musician and she is not a painter?

Chapter XX

Summary

Edna decides to visit Mademoiselle Reisz, despite the bad feeling she had gotten from their last conversation. She feels the need to hear her play the piano. Unfortunately, Mademoiselle Reisz has moved, and Edna has some trouble locating her. She decides to go to the Lebruns to ask Madame Lebrun. Victor answers the door, and after having an argument with his servant, he sends her to fetch Madame Lebrun.

Edna waits on the porch, and Victor sits down with her and amuses her with a story about a woman he had met the night before. Mrs. Lebrun comes out just as Victor is about to get into sordid details. She sends Victor in to get two letters from Robert to read to Edna. The letters are about his life in Mexico with no mention of Edna. She begins to feel despondent again and asks Madame Lebrun for Mademoiselle Reisz's address.

As she leaves, Edna banters a bit with Victor again and then regrets it, thinking she should have been more dignified and reserved. Mrs. Lebrun comments on how well she looks, and Victor notes that she seems like a different woman.

Analysis

Edna needs to see Mademoiselle Reisz, because she gives Edna inspiration and stirs her to feel passion, both of which Edna needs to keep going. Unfortunately she has a hard time finding her. Again we hear how unpleasant and unpopular Mademoiselle Reisz is, and this is because she is an artist who does not conform to society's rules and dictates. Her worst crime is that she is unmarried and childless. Adele naturally doesn't like her, because she is the polar opposite of Adele, who strictly conforms to society's standards and lives only for and through her family.

Victor's attitude is typical of his time. He can't tell Edna about his presumably raunchy adventures of the evening before because she is a woman and wouldn't understand. However, Edna has come a long way from the woman who blushed when Robert spoke of Adele's pregnancy. Her awakening sexuality and passion has taken over her inborn prudery, and she is interested and amused by Victor's story.

Edna begins to feel good until she reads Robert's letters, which make no mention of her. Then the feeling of despondency takes over, and she is reminded of her need to see Mademoiselle Reisz. Before she leaves, she banters with Victor again, before remembering that the proper thing would have been to look disapproving. But she is beyond such artifice and can respond only naturally now. Victor notices the change. He remarks that in "some way she doesn't seem like the same woman."

Study Questions

1. Why does Edna want to visit Mademoiselle Reisz?

2. Why does Edna have such a hard time finding Mademoiselle Reisz?

3. Why does it make sense that Adele wouldn't like Mademoiselle Reisz?

4. What does the Lebrun house remind Edna of?

5. Why is Victor fighting with the servant when he opens the door?

6. Why doesn't Victor want to tell Edna about the time he had the evening before?

7. Why does Victor grow more daring in the telling of his story?

8. Why do Robert's letters fill Edna with despondency?

9. What does Edna remember after she leaves Victor?

10. What does Victor perceive about Edna?

Answers

1. She wants to hear her play the piano; she wants to feel passion.

2. Mademoiselle Reisz moved, and since nobody liked her, nobody cared where she moved to.

3. Mademoiselle Reisz is the opposite of everything Adele believes in; she is unmarried, childless, and ugly.

4. It is like a prison because of the iron bars on the doors and lower windows.

5. The servant thought it was her job to open the door.

6. She is a woman and wouldn't comprehend such things.

7. Edna is showing interest in his story.

8. There is no message for her.

9. She remembers that she was supposed to be dignified and reserved.

10. He perceives that she has changed; he says she doesn't seem like the same woman.

Suggested Essay Topics

1. Describe the different influences Adele and Mademoiselle Reisz have upon Edna.

2. Describe the significance of Edna's bantering with Victor and how Edna has changed since she blushed at Robert's story in Chapter IV.

Chapter XXI

Summary

Mademoiselle Reisz lives in an apartment under the roof with open windows that let in soot and dirt along with the light and air. Everything is fairly dingy except for a "magnificent piano" that crowds the apartment.

Mademoiselle Reisz is glad to see Edna and expresses her surprise that Edna has actually come. As Mademoiselle Reisz pours coffee for them, she tells Edna she has a letter from Robert in which he writes of nothing but Edna. Edna asks to see it, but Mademoiselle Reisz refuses at first. Edna asks her to play the piano and tells her she has been painting, that she is becoming an artist. Mademoiselle Reisz replies that one must have more than talent to be a true artist; she said one must have a "courageous soul."

Mademoiselle Reisz finally agrees to let Edna see the letter, and she plays love songs on the piano while Edna reads. Edna begins to cry, just like the time Mademoiselle Reisz played at Grand Isle. When she leaves, she asks if she can come again.

Analysis

Mademoiselle Reisz's apartment, like her, is old and dingy and unkempt. However in the center of the apartment, crowding everything else, is a magnificent piano. True to her calling, nothing is important except her music.

Mademoiselle Reisz is pleased with Edna's honesty. There was a time when Edna would not have been so honest, but now she is not so afraid. It is part of her awakening, and in Mademoiselle Reisz's eyes, it is imperative if Edna is to become an artist.

When Edna tells Mademoiselle Reisz that she is becoming an artist, Mademoiselle Reisz is skeptical. She tells Edna that an artist must have a "courageous soul," one that is not afraid to defy convention. This Mademoiselle Reisz clearly has, and Adele clearly has not. Edna is beginning to develop a courageous soul but will never go so far as Mademoiselle Reisz.

Chopin again uses music and mysticism to set a romantic mood for Edna to read Robert's letter. Mademoiselle Reisz's music ranges from "quivering love notes" to "soulful and poignant longing." Then it becomes "strange and fantastic," spilling out from the deeply shadowed apartment up to the sky. Just as she did that night at Grand Isle, Edna bursts into tears.

Study Questions

1. What is the centerpiece of Mademoiselle Reisz's apartment?

2. How is Mademoiselle Reisz described when Edna sees her?

3. Why did Mademoiselle Reisz think that Edna would never come to visit?

4. Why is Mademoiselle Reisz pleased when Edna admits that she's not sure if she likes her?

5. What does Mademoiselle Reisz tell Edna about Robert's letter?

6. How does Edna describe herself to Mademoiselle Reisz?

7. What does Mademoiselle Reisz tell Edna about being an artist?

8. What did Mademoiselle Reisz play for Edna while Edna was reading Robert's letter?

9. What is Edna's reaction to the letter and the music?

10. How does Chopin set the mood for Edna's emotions?

Answers

1. She has a magnificent piano crowding everything else in the apartment.

2. She hasn't changed; she is the "little musician," still ugly, still wearing the same ugly dress.

3. Edna is a "society" woman, and those women generally have no use for artists such as Mademoiselle Reisz.

4. It is an honest answer and honesty takes courage.

5. The letter is all about Edna.

6. She says that she is becoming an artist.

7. She says that to be an artist one must have a courageous soul, a soul that dares and defies.

8. She starts with a song about longing, moves into a song about love, and then back into longing.

9. She begins to cry.

10. The music grows "fantastic" and fills the room, and the shadows deepen. There is a magical feeling.

Suggested Essay Topics

1. Why does an artist need a courageous soul? Why is it hard for women of that era to have that kind of courage? What is Edna doing to achieve a courageous soul?

2. How does Chopin use music to set the mood? How does the music interact with Edna's discovery of passion?

Chapter XXII

New Character:

Dr. Mandelet: *good doctor who tries to help Edna*

Summary

One morning Leonce decides to visit Dr. Mandelet, the family physician. He wants to talk about Edna, explaining that she is acting odd. He says that her whole attitude has changed and hints that they were no longer having sex. Dr. Mandelet inquires if Edna is spending time with a certain group of pseudointellectual women. Leonce explains that she has been isolated, not spending time with anyone. At this Dr. Mandelet grows concerned. Leonce tells him about Edna's sister's upcoming wedding and how Edna refuses to attend.

Dr. Mandelet advises Leonce to let Edna alone for a while, assuring him that this peculiarity would pass. He also agrees to come for dinner so he can observe Edna firsthand.

When Leonce leaves, Dr. Mandelet wonders to himself if there is another man in the picture.

Analysis

Dr. Mandelet is clearly a wise man. He is "known more for his wisdom than his skill," and his eyes "had lost none of their

penetration." However, he is still a man of his time and can understand only so much about Edna's awakening. When Leonce first explained Edna's strangeness, including that she refused to sleep with him, Dr. Mandelet thought she was mixed up with a group of "pseudointellectual women." It is only when Leonce tells him that Edna has been isolating that Dr. Mandelet becomes worried. This was very unnatural for a society woman. But even then he attributes it to the "moody and whimsical" nature of women and advises Leonce to ignore it until it has passed.

Dr. Mandelet secretly does wonder if Edna is having an affair. He knows, however, that this is something unheard of in the Creole culture so he wisely keeps quiet about it.

Study Questions

1. What kind of doctor is Dr. Mandelet?

2. Why does Leonce go to see Dr. Mandelet?

3. What is Edna's problem as Leonce describes it?

4. How is this most affecting Leonce?

5. What are Dr. Mandelet's first thoughts on Edna's problem?

6. Why does he finally get concerned?

7. Why won't Edna go to her sister's upcoming wedding?

8. What does Dr. Mandelet attribute Edna's problem to?

9. Why does Leonce invite Dr. Mandelet to dinner?

10. What is Dr. Mandelet's fear about Edna?

Answers

1. He is a semi-retired physician, known more for wisdom than skill.

2. He is worried about Edna.

3. She is suddenly concerned with women's rights and is therefore neglecting her family.

4. Edna has stopped sleeping with him.

5. He wonders if she has been associating with a certain group

of pseudointellectual women who might be putting ideas in her head.

6. Leonce tells him that she has been isolating, giving up her social ties.

7. She says that weddings are "one of the most lamentable spectacles on earth."

8. He says that women tend to get moody and whimsical and that this latest "mood" would probably pass.

9. He wants Dr. Mandelet to observe Edna firsthand.

10. He is afraid that there is another man involved in the picture.

Suggested Essay Topics

1. How are Dr. Mandelet's attitudes toward Edna's problem similar to Leonce's attitude?

2. How has Edna's awakening contributed to her refusal to sleep with her husband? How is this related to her comment that weddings are "one of the most lamentable spectacles on earth"?

Chapter XXIII

New Characters:

Alcee Arobin: *a young man-about-town with whom Edna has an affair*

The Highcamps and the Merrimans: *society people who are social friends of Edna's*

The Colonel: *Edna's father*

Summary

Edna's father is in the city to purchase a wedding gift for Edna's sister Janet. He is a retired colonel and still has his military bearing. Edna and her father are not very close but are companionable. He sits still for a sketch, happy to sit rigidly for hours.

Edna takes her father to a party at the Ratignolles' where Adele flirts with him. Edna notes that she is unable to do that. Leonce does not attend these parties; he prefers to be at the club. Adele expresses disapproval of this, but Edna is happy that they don't spend much time together. She wonders what they would talk about if they did.

One afternoon Edna and her father go to the racetrack, and win, and that is the main topic of conversation at dinner. At the track, they had met Mrs. Merriman, Mrs. Highcamp, and Alcee Arobin. Leonce, of course, disapproves of gambling. After dinner everyone tells stories. Edna tells one about a woman who had paddled away with a lover one night and never returned.

Dr. Mandelet is at dinner that night observing Edna, and he thinks Edna seems radiant. He notices a subtle change in her, a liveliness he had not seen before.

Analysis

The Colonel allows a glimpse into the other male influence on Edna. Her father is stern, rigid, and rugged; he wears padded jackets to make himself look bigger. When Edna is sketching him, he gets angry at the children for interrupting and disturbing his "fixed lines." In today's terms he would be called macho. He is certainly not someone who would be sympathetic to Edna's feelings.

Edna marvels at Adele's ability to flirt, noting that she cannot do so. This is because flirting is a feminine art, and Edna is consistently described as more masculine than feminine.

The sad truth of the Pontelliers' relationship is revealed when Adele says that Leonce should stay home more, and Edna is horrified, knowing that they would have nothing to say to one another. This is contrasted with the ease in which she converses with Robert and later Alcee Arobin.

Dr. Mandelet notices the change in Edna and uses very sexual terms to describe her. Although she used to be listless, she now seemed "palpitant with the forces of life" and like "some beautiful, sleek animal waking up in the sun." He becomes even more convinced that she is having an affair.

When Edna makes up the story about the woman who runs away with her lover, she is so passionate that it seems real to those who hear it; they could actually picture it in their minds.

Study Questions

1. What is the nature of Edna's relationship with her father?

2. Why is she glad he is visiting?

3. What does Edna's father look like?

4. Why can't Edna flirt like Adele?

5. Why does Leonce not attend the Ratignolles' parties?

6. How does Edna respond to Adele's suggestion that it would help the Pontelliers' relationship if Leonce stayed home more?

7. Why do Edna and her father have such a good time at the racetrack?

8. What does Dr. Mandelet think of Edna when he comes to dinner?

9. Why is Edna's story significant?

10. What does Dr. Mandelet think about Edna's problem after observing her?

Answers

1. Edna is not warmly attached to her father, but they are companionable because they have certain tastes in common.

2. He provides a distraction and a new outlet for her emotions.

3. He is tall and thin, with silky white hair and moustache. He still has his military bearing and wears jackets that exaggerate the breadth of his chest.

4. Edna has been too repressed to play such games. She is also too masculine for such "girlish" games.

5. He would rather spend his time with the men at the club.

6. Edna would be very unhappy if Leonce were home more often. She says that they would have nothing to talk about.

7. They won money and met some charming people, including Alcee Arobin.

8. He notices that she seems to have come to life, and she reminds him of a sleek animal waking up in the sun.

9. She is hinting at her inclinations, perhaps looking for a response to the idea.

10. He is even more sure that another man was involved.

Suggested Essay Topics

1. How does Dr. Mandelet's description of Edna fit in with her awakening? How does this imagery compare with other natural imagery Chopin uses?

2. Why doesn't Adele understand Edna's contentment with Leonce's spending time away from her?

Chapter XXIV

Summary

Edna and her father have a fight over Edna's refusal to attend her sister's wedding. Leonce, on Dr. Mandelet's advice, stays out of it, but he plans to go himself to atone for Edna. Edna's father disapproves of the way Leonce is handling the situation. He advises him to put his foot down, asserting that "authority and coercion" were necessary to handle a wife. Even Leonce realizes that the Colonel had probably coerced his own wife into an early grave. Edna is very glad when he leaves.

Just before Leonce leaves for New York shortly thereafter, Edna grows affectionate and feels she will miss him. The children leave, too, off to stay with their grandmother in the country. When Edna is finally alone, a "radiant peace" settles over her. She feels a new and "delicious" feeling. She walks through the house as if she is seeing it for the first time. She enjoys a solitary dinner and then reads Emerson in the library until she grows sleepy. When she finally snuggles beneath her covers, she feels a restfulness she had not known before.

Analysis

In the preceding chapter, we learned a bit about Edna's father. Now we learn something about her mother. When the Colonel advises Leonce that "authority and coercion" are needed to manage a wife, we are told that the Colonel was "perhaps unaware that he had coerced his own wife into her grave." This could mean either that she became sick and died or, more portentiously, maybe she committed suicide. In any event it becomes more and more clear what Edna has been up against all her life and how difficult her journey is.

Edna grew somewhat sentimental before Leonce left, acting like a true wife for a while. However, once he and the children were gone, she felt a "radiant peace" and a feeling of relief. She views her house as if for the first time. In a way it is the first time because she is a different person. She is looking at the house as if it were hers instead of Leonce's, and therefore she is enjoying it.

As always, Edna enjoys her food. This is another sensual image: Edna's constant satisfying of her physical appetite. It is also something that sets her apart from other women who usually pretend not to enjoy their food.

Study Questions

1. What is Leonce's position in Edna's fight with her father over her sister's wedding?

2. What is the Colonel's advice to Leonce about Edna?

3. What is hinted at about the Colonel's wife?

4. How does Edna feel right before Leonce leaves for a long trip to New York?

5. How does she actually feel after Leonce and the children have gone?

6. What does she do when she is finally alone?

7. What is Edna's first meal alone like?

8. What does Edna do after dinner?

9. What does Edna plan to do now that she is on her own?

10. How does Edna feel as she snuggles in her bed at night?

Answers

1. Leonce, on Dr. Mandelet's advice, stays out of it.

2. He says that authority and coercion are needed to manage a wife.

3. It is hinted that maybe she had committed suicide.

4. She feels almost affectionate and thinks that she will miss him.

5. A radiant peace settles over her, a feeling of relief.

6. She walks through the house as if it were the first time, enjoying everything as never before.

7. She enjoys a tasty meal with good wine and the comfort of being able to dine in a peignoir.

8. She reads in the library until she grows sleepy.

9. She wants to embark on a course of intellectual self-improvement.

10. She feels a sense of restfulness that she has never known before.

Suggested Essay Topics

1. Imagine that you are Edna but are allowed to speak freely. How would you respond to the Colonel's statement that authority and coercion are needed to manage a wife?

2. Why does Edna walk through the house as if it were the first time? How is the house different for her now?

Chapter XXV

Summary

Edna cannot work when it is dark and cloudy; she needs the sunlight to inspire her. On rainy days she goes out to see friends or sits home alone feeling as if her life is passing her by.

She begins frequenting the racetrack. One afternoon, Mrs. Highcamp and Alcee Arobin invited her to the track. She plays for very high stakes and wins; she feels intoxicated.

After dinner at the Highcamps, Alcee drives Edna home, and she agrees to go to the races with him again. After Alcee leaves,

Edna feels hungry, restless, and excited. She wants something exciting to happen and regrets she did not ask Alcee to stay and talk for a while.

A few days later Alcee calls on Edna to go to the races, and this time they go alone. She feels excited again and becomes easily intimate with Alcee, who is good at initiating such intimacy. He stays for dinner, and afterward they sit by the fire. He shows Edna a scar on his wrist, and she touches his hand as she looks at it. Then she jumps up and walks away, agitated.

Alcee walks back over to her, and she feels an awakening sensuousness as she looks at him. He sees it and feels emboldened to take her hand when he says goodnight.

However, when Alcee asks if she will go to the races again, she says no and tells him to leave, saying that she doesn't like him; they both know she is lying. He kisses her hand, and she explains that she was excited from the track and hopes she hadn't misled him. He also apologizes and finally leaves.

After Alcee left, Edna stares at her hand where he kissed her. She feels like she had already been unfaithful and wonders what Robert would think of it. She knows she doesn't really care for Alcee, yet his presence and his touch act as a "narcotic" upon her. She falls into a deep sleep.

Analysis

As Edna becomes more independent, she grows more confident in herself as an artist. Yet it is not enough, and there are days when she feels her life is passing her by.

Mrs. Highcamp is a married woman who has affairs with young men. She attracts them through her young daughter and then seeks them for herself. She is a route Edna will later choose not to go.

One place Edna feels young and alive is at the racetrack. She wins a lot of money and feels intoxicated. Chopin often describes Edna as feeling intoxicated when she feels powerful.

After spending the whole day with the purposefully charming Alcee, Edna feels restless and excited. She wants something to happen. She doesn't realize it yet, but Alcee stirred a passion in her. When they finally spend some time alone together, it becomes more clear. Alcee, who is used to seducing women, gets Edna to

touch his hand by showing her a scar on his wrist. Her own response flusters her though, and she walks away from him. She tries to send him away, telling him she doesn't like him, but it is too late. After he leaves, she stares at her hand where he kissed it good-bye and feels like she was already unfaithful. This is because of what she is thinking and feeling about Alcee.

Study Questions

1. Why can't Edna work when it's dark and cloudy?

2. How does Edna feel on her melancholy days?

3. What does Alcee look like?

4. Why does Edna enjoy the racetrack so much?

5. How does Edna feel while she is at the track?

6. How does Edna feel after Alcee takes her home?

7. What happens between Edna and Alcee at the track?

8. Why does Edna touch Alcee's hand?

9. What happens when Alcee looks into Edna's eyes?

10. What is Edna's reaction to Alcee after he has gone?

Answers

1. She needs the sun to mellow her mood.

2. She feels as if her life is passing her by, leaving her with broken and unfulfilled promises.

3. He has a good body, a pleasant face not burdened with any depth of thought or feeling, a perpetual smile in his eyes, and he dresses in the height of fashion.

4. It reminds her of happy times in her childhood stables. Also, she wins a lot of money.

5. She feels intoxicated.

6. She wanted something exciting to happen and regretted that she had not asked him to stay a while.

7. They develop a certain intimacy.

8. He is showing her a scar on his wrist.

9. He draws out all her latent sensuality.

10. She stares at her hand where he kissed her goodnight and feels like she has already been unfaithful.

Suggested Essay Topics

1. How does Edna's experience at the track compare with other experiences where she felt intoxicated? What is the meaning of this intoxication?

2. Why does Edna allow Alcee to kiss her hand? Why does she then feel like she has been unfaithful?

Chapter XXVI

Summary

Alcee writes Edna a note of apology, and Edna feels silly for having made a fuss over a kiss on the hand. Soon they are spending time together again, growing closer and more intimate. Sometimes he talks in a way that makes her blush, but after a while she enjoys it; there is something in her that responds to it.

When Edna needs a lift, she visits Mademoiselle Reisz; her music "seemed to reach Edna's spirit and set it free." Upon arriving at Mademoiselle Reisz's apartment, Edna informs her that she is moving out of her house to a smaller one around the corner. When pressed for a reason, Edna says it is because she wants a place of her own. She has her own money now because of her winnings at the track and from sales of her paintings. She has resolved never to "belong" to anyone again. Edna also tells Mademoiselle Reisz that she is giving a dinner party the night before she leaves the old house.

Mademoiselle Reisz gives another of Robert's letters to Edna to read. She tells Edna that the reason he doesn't write her is because he is in love with her and is trying to forget her because she is not free. Edna reads as Mademoiselle Reisz's music brightens her soul, "preparing her for joy and exultation"; the letter says Robert is coming home soon.

Edna finally admits to Mademoiselle Reisz that she is in love with Robert, although she can't explain why. She feels suddenly happy, knowing he is coming home. On her way home, she stops at a confectioners to send a box of candy to her children. Then she writes a cheerful letter to Leonce, telling him of her intention to move out.

Analysis

Alcee has wormed his way into Edna's life, and they are growing more and more intimate. She is getting used to having him around the way she got used to having Robert around, although she doesn't feel the same way about Alcee. Edna likes having adoring men around her. In Chapter VI she says of Leonce that "his absolute devotion flattered her." So although she is seeking and gaining independence, she does not want to be totally alone. It is important to her to have a man around, which is why she cannot become like Mademoiselle Reisz.

Alcee continues to bring out Edna's sexuality, talking to her in ways that make her blush at first, but soon please her, "appealing to the animalism that stirred impatiently within her."

Edna visits Mademoiselle Reisz and tells her that she is moving from her house into a smaller one around the corner because she wants it to be hers completely. She has been gaining not only emotional independence but financial independence through her winnings at the track and sales of her paintings. This financial independence can buy her physical independence. It also takes her farther away from being a traditional woman; financial independence was usually reserved for men.

Mademoiselle Reisz tells Edna that Robert is coming home and that he is in love with her. Then Edna admits her own feelings for him. One wonders why Mademoiselle Reisz is so interested in Robert and Edna; perhaps it is because she has no love in her own life.

When Edna leaves Mademoiselle Reisz's, she sends her children a box of candy along with a loving note. As usual she feels loving toward her children when she feels happy and fulfilled with her own life.

Study Questions

1. Why does Edna deliberate over how to answer Alcee's apology?

2. Why is it so easy for Alcee to become intimate with Edna?

3. Why does Edna visit Mademoiselle Reisz?

4. Why do you think Mademoiselle Reisz is always eating or drinking chocolate?

5. What reason does Edna give for moving out of her house?

6. How does Edna have the money to be on her own?

7. What is Edna's big resolve?

8. Why does Edna sigh after announcing her farewell dinner party?

9. What good news does Edna find out from Mademoiselle Reisz?

10. Why does Edna send a box of candy to her children?

Answers

1. Edna doesn't want to give it undue importance, and she doesn't want him to think she took it seriously.

2. He appeals to the sexual self that is awakening inside her.

3. Mademoiselle Reisz, through her music, touches Edna's spirit and makes her feel free and hopeful.

4. Her life is bitter and alone, and chocolate is sweet.

5. She wants a place that is her own, not provided for by her husband.

6. She has been winning a lot of money at the track and selling some of her paintings. Additionally, she has a small inheritance from her mother.

7. She vows that she will never again belong to another person.

8. It is clear to her that she has never really been happy.

9. She learns that Robert loves her and that he is coming home soon.

10. When Edna is happy, she feels more loving toward her children.

Suggested Essay Topics

1. What is the significance of Edna's moving into her own house? Why is it so important for her to have this physical separation?

2. Why is it that Edna feels more loving toward her children when she feels happy with herself? How do the children affect her desire for independence?

Chapters XXVII and XXVIII

Summary

That evening, in Chapter XXVII, Alcee says he has never seen Edna in such a good mood. He sits close to her, letting his fingers lightly touch her hair, which she enjoys. Then she tells Alcee she needs to figure out what kind of woman she is; she feels wicked but doesn't really think she is. Alcee responds that she needn't think about it because he can tell her what kind of woman she is.

Then Edna recounts something Mademoiselle Reisz had said to her about how birds that want to soar above tradition and prejudice must have strong wings. Alcee responds that Mademoiselle Reisz must be demented, but Edna argues that she seems wonderfully sane to her.

Alcee notes that Edna's thoughts seem far away, then leans over and kisses her on the lips. She clasps his head, holding his lips to hers. It is the first kiss of her life that arouses her.

Chapter XXVIII is the second narrative break of the novel. Chopin tells us that Edna cried a bit after Alcee left. She felt irresponsible, and she felt the reproaches of Leonce and Robert. However, she also felt that she understood the world a little better. She did not feel any shame or remorse, only regret that it was not the kiss of love that had inflamed her.

Analysis

In Chapter XXVII, Edna knows that by society's standards she is wicked because she is in love with another man and wants to leave her husband. Yet she doesn't feel wicked because, for the first time in her life, she is following her heart and being true to herself. We see here how Alcee is no different from Leonce or any other man. He tells Edna he can tell her about herself better than she can. He is already assuming a proprietary "I know best" air with her.

He also clearly doesn't understand what she is trying to do with her life; his only response to Mademoiselle Reisz's comment is that he heard she was demented. Mademoiselle Reisz is the only one who truly understands Edna and the only one who understands how difficult her journey is; even Edna doesn't quite get that yet. Mademoiselle Reisz knows how difficult it is to defy convention and rise above prejudice.

When Alcee kisses Edna, she feels aroused for the first time in her life.

In Chapter XXVIII, Edna is filled with emotion after being with Alcee. She knows that Leonce would feel betrayed because of all the material things he has provided her with. She thinks Robert would feel betrayed because she gave herself for less than true love. However, Edna now understands the difference between lust and love and does not feel ashamed of her lust. It is crucial that she does not feel shame or remorse; this is because she is responding to her true nature, one she has denied her whole life. She feels that anything she does now is acceptable. The only regret she has is that it was Alcee and not Robert who is her true love.

Study Questions

1. Why does Edna say she is a wicked woman?
2. Why does she think at the same time that she is not?
3. What is Alcee's response to Edna's question?
4. What is significant about Alcee's response?
5. What does Mademoiselle Reisz tell Edna about courage?
6. How does Edna feel after kissing Alcee?

7. What is the significance of the reproach Edna imagines from Robert?

8. What does Edna understand about life after being with Alcee?

9. What specifically does Edna not feel?

10. Why does Edna feel a pang of regret?

Answers

1. Edna knows she would be perceived as wicked because of her move toward independence and because of the sexual feelings she has.

2. She is following her true nature.

3. He says she shouldn't bother thinking about it because he can tell her what kind of woman she is.

4. He is acting just like any other man, presuming to know better than she does, not letting her be independent.

5. She says that Edna must have a lot of strength and courage if she is going to defy convention and prejudice.

6. It is the first kiss of her life that truly arouses her.

7. It is because she is giving herself for less than true love.

8. She realizes that there is a difference between lust and love.

9. She does not feel either shame or regret.

10. She wishes that it was love, rather than lust, that had opened her up.

Suggested Essay Topics

1. Why doesn't Edna feel shame or regret? In Chapter VI, Chopin talked about wisdom that is usually denied to women. What is Edna learning from being with Alcee, and why is that usually denied to women?

2. Describe the reactions that Leonce, Robert, Mademoiselle Reisz, and Adele would have to Edna's actions.

Chapter XXIX

Summary

Without waiting for an answer from Leonce regarding her decision to move, Edna hastens her plans. There is no thought involved, she just moves. She takes only what is hers. Alcee arrives in the afternoon, walking in unannounced, and finds Edna on a stepladder taking a picture off the wall. He then helps out. She tells him the dinner party will be two days later with the very finest of everything; she is going to let Leonce pay for it. She says goodbye to Alcee, and he is dismayed that he can't see her again before the party.

Analysis

Edna hastens her preparations to move out after spending the night with Alcee. She realizes now more than ever her need for independence. Now that she's experienced such pleasure she wants to be able to continue, and she can't do that in the old house. In fact the old house now seems forbidden, as if she had desecrated an altar.

Edna is determined to be completely independent, and so she takes nothing that belongs to Leonce. Her independence is underscored by Alcee's reflection that she never looked more handsome. She is more masculine because she is freer.

Alcee continues to act in a proprietary manner. He walks in the house unannounced as if he lived there. Being such a womanizer, he probably expected Edna to be either tearful or ashamed. He has no idea who or what he's dealing with.

Edna's allowing Leonce to pay the bills for the party seems a bit out of character, but it's probably a final bit of revenge.

Study Questions

1. How does Edna go about her preparations to move?

2. What is causing Edna to be in such a rush?

3. What does Edna mean when she says the old house seems like a forbidden temple?

4. What does Edna take from the old house to the new?

5. How does Alcee enter the house?

6. How does Alcee expect to find Edna after their night together?

7. What is Edna doing when Alcee walks in the house?

8. How is Edna described when she is up on the stepladder?

9. What is significant about this description of Edna?

10. Why does Alcee call Edna's dinner a coup d'état?

Answers

1. She moves feverishly, with no deliberation before action.

2. Her night with Alcee increases her desire to be on her own.

3. It is someplace where she is an intruder and no longer has a right to be.

4. She takes only what belongs solely to her, not bought by Leonce.

5. He rings but then walks right in.

6. He expects her to be either angry or sentimental, not indifferent.

7. She is on a stepladder unhooking a picture from the wall.

8. She never appeared more handsome.

9. It can be taken to mean she never looked more masculine, in the sense of what she is doing rather than how she actually looks.

10. He means that it is her farewell dinner from Leonce's house, and she is letting Leonce pay the bills for it.

Suggested Essay Topics

1. What does it say about Edna that she is letting Leonce pay the bills for her dinner? Is this consistent with her character so far?

2. What is the significance of Alcee's walking in the house, unannounced?

Chapter XXX

Summary

Edna's dinner party and its guests are described in detail. There are nine guests, and Edna seats herself between Alcee and Mademoiselle Reisz. The table is set lavishly, with satin, lace, silver, gold, and crystal. There are fresh red and yellow roses on the table.

The conversation is lively and loud, and the food is abundant. Mrs. Highcamp, seated next to Victor Lebrun, spends the evening trying to capture his attention.

Edna is dressed in satin and is wearing a diamond tiara, a birthday present from Leonce which had arrived that morning. Edna is 29 years old. Seated at the head of the table, her bearing is regal. Yet she feels her old ennui creeping in, and seeing Robert's picture before her eyes, feels overwhelmed with helplessness.

Monsieur Ratignolle is the first to leave; Adele was at home, anxious about her impending birth. Mademoiselle Reisz goes with him.

Mrs. Highcamp begins increasing her attention to Victor, draping him first with a garland of roses and then a white scarf. Victor, a bit drunk from the wine and the attention, agrees to sing. However, the song he chooses was the one his brother Robert had sung to Edna on the boat. Edna shouts out for him to stop. In the process, she spills a glass of wine on Alcee and Mrs. Highcamp. Victor, unfortunately, doesn't take her seriously at first, and Edna has to get up and cover his mouth with her hand. After this incident, everyone leaves except Alcee.

Analysis

Edna plans her farewell dinner party to be her moment of glory. She spares no expense with the food or the table setting. In fact, she looks like a queen sitting at the head of her table. By all accounts her party is a smashing success. The irony is that Edna becomes miserably unhappy during the meal, realizing that all she wants is Robert and nothing else matters.

Mrs. Highcamp's attempted seduction of Victor is important to Edna's decision to kill herself. Mrs. Highcamp is seen as pathetic,

using her daughter as a pretext to seduce young men. Edna knows that if she stays married to Leonce for the sake of her children, she could end up like Mrs. Highcamp. That thought is horrifying and degrading to her.

Edna is so absorbed in her newfound sexuality that even as she forces Victor to stop singing because it reminds her of Robert, she still notices how good his lips feels on her hand.

Study Questions

1. Why is Adele unable to attend Edna's dinner party?
2. Describe the splendor of the dinner table.
3. How does Edna appear, sitting at the head of the table?
4. Why is the occasion doubly special for Edna?
5. Despite all the glamour, how does Edna feel?
6. Why is Alcee's name on the letterhead of a law firm?
7. What does Mrs. Highcamp do to Victor, and what does she want?
8. What song does Victor sing at the table?
9. What is Edna's reaction?
10. What does Edna have to do to get Victor to stop singing?

Answers

1. She is close to giving birth and in a lot of pain.
2. The tablecloth is pale yellow satin under strips of lace. There are candles in brass candelabra, fresh roses, silver, gold, and crystal.
3. With her dress of satin and lace and her diamond tiara, she appears regal, in control, alone.
4. It is her twenty-ninth birthday.
5. She feels tired and hopeless, thinking about Robert with longing.
6. He finds it necessary to "assume the virtue of an occupation" to satisfy other people's inquiries.

7. She weaves a garland of roses and places it on his head, then drapes his shoulders with a white silk scarf. She is trying to seduce him.

8. He sings the song that Robert sang to Edna on the boat.

9. She cries out for him to stop and is so upset that she spills a glass of wine.

10. She walks behind him and puts her hand over his mouth.

Suggested Essay Topics

1. What does Mrs. Highcamp's behavior tell Edna about her choices in life? Knowing what you know about Edna so far, do you think she would want to stay married to Leonce and have affairs?

2. Why does Chopin take such great pains to describe the splendor of the party? Explain Edna's sadness.

Chapter XXXI

New Character:

Celestine: *the Pontelliers' servant*

Summary

After everyone leaves, Edna and Alcee lock up and leave for the new house. Celestine, the Pontelliers' servant, is moving in with Edna into the new house but will go back and clean up at the old house in the morning. Edna is quiet and seems disheartened.

When they arrive at the new house, it feels homey and hospitable; Edna had been working on it already. It is also filled with flowers that Alcee had sent over earlier.

Edna tells Alcee that she feels tired and miserable and that she just wants to rest. She puts her head down on the table, and Alcee begins stroking her hair, then moves to her shoulders. Finally, he sits down and kisses her. When she says she thought he was leaving, he replies that he will after he says good night. However, he does not leave until after they make love.

Analysis

Edna feels disheartened after her party, wanting nothing but
to be alone (since Robert is not available). She is happy to go to
her new house, which she has already made homey and hospitable.
This is in direct contrast to the old house, which was telling her to
go away.

Despite Edna's stated intention to be alone, Alcee's magnetic
hands draw her in and she follows the desires of her body. It is as if
she no longer cares, and for the moment, she is willing to settle for
second best. Her desire to feel *something*, to experience whatever
life has to offer, outweighs the emptiness she feels with Alcee.

Study Questions

1. Where does Edna go after her party?
2. How does Alcee act around Edna now?
3. What does Edna mean when Alcee offers her a spray of jes-
   samine, and she says she doesn't want anything?
4. What does Edna notice as she and Alcee walk to the new house?
5. What is the surprise waiting for Edna at her new house?
6. How does the parlor in the new house look when they enter?
7. How does Alcee's touch on Edna's hair feel?
8. Why does Edna say the party was stupid?
9. What does Alcee notice when he touches Edna's shoulder?
10. How does the evening end for Edna and Alcee?

Answers

1. She goes over to her new house.
2. He acts like a husband.
3. All she wants is Robert, and nothing else is really important.
4. She notices the way his leg moves so close to her and how
   the black of his pants looks against the yellow of her gown.

5. Alcee has filled the house with fresh flowers.

6. It looks homey and hospitable.

7. It is magnetic, and it draws her in.

8. She now thinks it was stupid because it didn't make her happy like she thought it would.

9. Alcee notices that her body is responding sexually.

10. They spend the night together.

Suggested Essay Topics

1. Why does Edna sleep with Alcee when she's longing for Robert?

2. Explain the irony of the term "pigeon-house." What makes the new house seem so homey and hospitable, and why is that so important to Edna?

Chapter XXXII

Summary

Leonce, who is too late, sends word to Edna that he disapproves of her move, mainly because he is afraid that people will think their finances have taken a turn for the worse. He takes care of it in a businesslike manner, immediately planning reconstruction of the old house so that it will seem like they had no choice but to move.

Edna is very happy in her new home. She feels that although she may have descended the social scale, she has moved up on the spiritual scale and is able to see and understand things with her own eyes.

Edna goes to visit her children who are staying with Leonce's mother on the farm. She weeps with joy to see them and truly enjoys their company for the whole week. When she leaves, she carries the sound of their voices all the way home. However, once she gets home, she forgets it, because she is alone again.

Analysis

As always, Leonce's concerns are financial, not personal. His only thought over Edna's moving out is how it might affect his reputation and his business.

Edna enjoys her new home and feels as if she has grown spiritually. She is seeing the world with new eyes—with her own eyes—and she is thinking rather than blindly accepting. She is understanding things in a whole new way, gaining wisdom that most women never gain (see Chapter VI). Maybe she had to descend socially to do this because in her old social world it would not be possible. In her old social world, one had to conform to be accepted.

Because Edna is feeling spiritually fulfilled and independent, she feels loving toward her children and can't get enough of them. Continuing with the theme of fulfilling appetite, Edna feels "hungry" for her children. Of course as soon as she returns home, she forgets them again.

It becomes clear that, as she has been accused of before, Edna has not thought out her future. What will she do when it is time for Leonce and the children to return? She tells the children that "the fairies would fix it all right," but that is part of her fantasy. She thinks everything will work out if she just keeps on her present course. She does not yet realize the full implications and possible consequences of her actions.

Study Questions

1. What is Leonce's main concern with Edna's moving out of the house?

2. What specifically is Leonce not concerned about?

3. How does Leonce handle Edna's move?

4. How does Edna feel about her new home?

5. What does Edna's "spiritual awakening" feel like to her?

6. How does Edna feel when she goes to visit her children?

7. What does Edna give to her children?

8. How does Edna respond to the children's concerns about their place in the new house?

9.   How does Edna feel when she leaves the children?

10. How does she feel when she returns home?

Answers

1.   He is afraid people would think the Pontelliers' finances had taken a turn for the worse, and this could hurt him financially.

2.   He is not concerned about scandal. It never occurs to him that Edna might have another man.

3.   He takes care of it in a businesslike manner, hiring an architect to remodel his home so that it would look like Edna had no choice but to move out for a while. He also puts a notice in the paper to that effect.

4.   She is very happy there and feels that although she may have descended on the social scale, she has clearly risen on the spiritual scale.

5.   She begins to see things with her own eyes, and to have a deeper understanding of life.

6.   She is so happy she weeps for joy. She feels hungry for them and is happy to listen to their stories.

7.   She gives them all of herself, for the first time ever.

8.   She tells them the fairies will fix everything all right.

9.   Edna feels sad when she leaves the children and carries away with her the sound of their voices and the touch of their cheeks.

10. As soon as Edna is alone in her new house again, she forgets once more about her children.

Suggested Essay Topics

1.   What is the significance of Edna's telling her children the fairies will fix everything all right? What does this say about Edna's plans for the future?

2. Why is it that to rise on the spiritual scale Edna needs to descend on the social scale? Give examples of both her social descent and her spiritual ascent.

Chapter XXXIII

Summary

One day, Edna sets out for Mademoiselle Reisz's to rest and talk about Robert. She had a talk with Adele earlier in the day, and Adele had noted that Edna seemed to act without reflection—like a little child. She worried what people would think about Alcee's visits. Then she made Edna promise that she would come when Adele gives birth.

Edna is waiting in Mademoiselle Reisz's apartment for the lady to come home and begins to softly play the piano. There is a knock on the door, and Edna says to come in. It is Robert; he clasps her hand. Then Edna sits by the window, and Robert sits on the piano stool. He tells Edna he has been home for two days. She is very upset and wonders if he really loves her, as Mademoiselle Reisz had said. He stammers some excuse about why he hasn't been to see her.

Edna sees in Robert's eyes the same feelings that had always been there, but neither one say anything. He is surprised that Edna is not away with her husband or her children.

They leave together without waiting for Mademoiselle Reisz to return, and Edna asks him to stay for dinner. He tries to get out of it but ends up staying. At the house he sees a picture of Alcee and asks a lot of questions; he clearly disapproves of Edna spending time with him. Robert reports that he has been feeling like a lost soul; Edna echoes the feeling. Then they become silent and wait for Celestine to serve dinner.

Analysis

Adele's pregnancy has been a theme throughout the novel, and it is no surprise that it will end up having a major impact on Edna. Here Edna promises Adele that she will go to her at any hour of the day or night, and the reader should guess by now that something

important will happen there.

Edna's and Robert's meeting takes place in Mademoiselle Reisz's apartment, the place where Edna found out Robert loved her and admitted that she loved him. However, the meeting is not as Edna fantasized it. Again she does not think about reality at this point, only about what she wants. She does not think at all about how Robert, an honorable Creole man, would feel about taking a married woman away from her husband.

Edna is glad that Robert did not know her in her old house because that was her fake self; she wants Robert to know her as she truly is, a woman free to love.

Robert has no sense of Edna's awakening, which is why he thinks she is mocking him when she mimics his answer. To his mind, she is not a free woman and therefore should not be having feelings for him. He still doesn't know that she loves him.

Study Questions

1. Why does Edna want to visit Mademoiselle Reisz?

2. What does Adele make Edna promise before she leaves her?

3. What does Adele warn Edna about?

4. Why is Edna caught off guard when Robert tells her he has been home for two days?

5. What reason does Robert give for coming home?

6. What does Edna see when she looks into Robert's eyes?

7. Why is Edna glad that Robert never knew her in her former home?

8. What does Robert mean when he said he's been "seeing the waves and the white beach of Grand Isle"?

9. Why does Edna mimic Robert's answer?

10. Why does Robert say that Edna is cruel?

Answers

1. She wants to rest and talk about Robert.

2. Adele makes Edna promise that she would go to her when she goes into labor, no matter what time of the day or night.

3. She warns her that Alcee has a bad reputation and that people might start talking about the two of them.

4. Edna expected that Robert would seek her out immediately after returning home.

5. He was having trouble with the Mexicans, and he was not making the money he thought he would.

6. She sees that he still loves her.

7. Edna doesn't like the person she was when she lived with Leonce.

8. He means that he has been thinking about Edna.

9. She wants him to understand that she feels the same way about him.

10. He thinks she is mocking him, because she is married and not free to love him.

Suggested Essay Topics

1. Explain from Robert's point of view why he hadn't called on Edna since his return. Compare this with the time they spent together at Grand Isle and explain why he felt freer then.

2. How is Edna different in her new house than in the old one? Why would she not have wanted Robert to know her in the old house?

Chapter XXXIV

Summary

The dining room is small and intimate, but dinner makes them both more formal. They talk about what they have been doing since they last met. After dinner Robert goes out to get cigarette paper. Edna notices that his tobacco pouch is new, and Robert admits that a girl gave it to him. Edna asks him lots of jealous questions, but he says the woman wasn't important.

Robert says Edna can throw him out any time, but Edna reminds him of all the time they spent together in Grand Isle. Robert responds that he remembers everything from Grand Isle.

Then Alcee drops in, and Robert takes that as a cue to leave. Edna tells Alcee to leave. Alcee does not want to leave but compiles with Edna' request. After Alcee leaves, Edna falls into a stupor thinking about the hours she has just spent with Robert. She feels that they had actually been closer when he was still in Mexico.

Analysis

Edna is desperately trying to win Robert over, and Robert is just as desperately trying to remain aloof, although he makes his feelings clear when he says, without looking at her, "I have forgotten nothing about Grand Isle." Still he leaves at the first opportunity, which is when Alcee arrives.

Edna wants to be alone to think about Robert so she sends Alcee away. Alcee has always been a womanizer so it is ironic when he says to Edna of his stated devotion, "I have said it before, but I don't think I ever came so near meaning it." Alcee feels no more for Edna than she does for him. It is physical, nothing more.

Edna falls into a stupor when they leave. Her stupors are contrasted throughout the novel with her feelings of intoxication. She feels intoxicated when she feels powerful, and she goes into a stupor when she feels hopeless or powerless. She feels powerless with Robert now because their reunion had not been all she had hoped for, and all she can do now is wait.

Study Questions

1. What happens when Robert and Edna sit down to eat dinner?

2. Why does Celestine spend time talking to Robert?

3. Why does Robert go out during dinner?

4. Why is Robert looking to leave when he says perhaps he shouldn't have come back?

5. What does Robert say in response to Edna's remembrance of all the time they spent together at Grand Isle?

6. Why does Edna pick up Robert's tobacco pouch?

7. How does Alcee's appearance affect the evening?

8. Why does Edna send Alcee away to mail a letter?

9. How does Edna feel after Alcee leaves?

10. How does Edna feel about Robert being home?

Answers

1. A degree of ceremony settles in during dinner, and they make small talk that has nothing to do with their feelings for each other.

2. Celestine knew Robert when he was a child, and besides, she is very interested in what is going on.

3. He goes out to get cigarette papers.

4. Robert is uncomfortable because of his feelings for Edna and feels safer when he is not with her.

5. He says that he has forgotten nothing about Grand Isle.

6. She picks up his tobacco pouch because it is new, and she is jealous of whomever gave it to him.

7. Robert leaves after Alcee arrives.

8. Edna wants to be alone with her thoughts of Robert.

9. She feels as if she is in a stupor.

10. She feels that in some ways she was closer to him when he was in Mexico.

Suggested Essay Topics

1. Why does Edna feel further away from Robert now that he is home?

2. Why does Edna send Alcee away? What is different this night than the night in Chapter XXXI?

Chapter XXXV

Summary

Edna wakes up filled with hope. She believes that Robert's love for her will surmount his reserve, whatever his reasons for it. She imagines him coming over that evening.

She receives letters from her children and from Leonce. Leonce writes that when he comes back they would take a trip abroad, as he had recently made a lot of money on Wall Street. She also receives a letter from Alcee saying good morning and assuring her of his devotion.

Edna writes back to the children and to Leonce. In Leonce's letter she is evasive, not on purpose, but because she had lost a sense of reality. She feels she has abandoned herself to Fate. She does not answer Alcee's letter.

Robert does not come that day, and Edna is very disappointed. Nor does he come either of the next two days. She would awake with hope and go to sleep despondent. However she does not seek him out; in fact she avoids places where he might be.

She goes out with Alcee one night, and they come back to Edna's to eat. It is late when he leaves. Since their relationship has become sexual, it has become a habit for him to spend time with her. That night she does not feel despondent when she goes to sleep, but neither does she wake up with any hope.

Analysis

Edna has completely lost sight of reality in the beginning of this chapter. She wakes up filled with hope and sees before her no denial; she still believes she will get everything she wants with no consequences.

She is also still being completely selfish. She doesn't care why Robert is being reserved. She is only interested in how she can break down that reserve.

After Robert does not come for a few days, Edna is willing to settle for Alcee and spends the night with him. That is when she gives up both despondency and hope, feeling nothing.

Study Questions

1. How does Edna feel when she wakes up?

2. How does she plan to melt Robert's reserve?

3. What does she daydream about?

4. From whom does Edna receive letters that morning?

5. How does Edna answer Leonce's letter?

6. What does Edna do with Alcee's letter?

7. How does Edna's next few days pass?

8. What does Edna do to try to see Robert?

9. Why does Edna enjoy the fastness of her ride with Alcee?

10. How do Edna's feelings change after not seeing Robert for a few days?

Answers

1. The morning is filled with sunlight and hope, and she imagines having everything she wants come true.

2. She believes that her passion will win him over.

3. She imagines Robert's day, from his walk to work, to the evening when he would come to see her.

4. She receives letters from Roaul, Leonce, and Alcee.

5. She answers it evasively because she is living in her fantasy world now and feels she is being driven along by Fate. Therefore she can't answer any of Leonce's questions about the future.

6. She doesn't respond to Alcee's letter.

7. She wakes up hopeful about seeing Robert and goes to sleep despondent over not having seen him.

8. She does nothing and in fact avoids places where she might run into him accidentally.

9. It is important to Edna to feel something and that feeling of recklessness would be a good temporary substitute for what she wants to feel.

10. She no longer feels despondency or hope.

Suggested Essay Topics

1. How do we know Edna is no longer living in the real world? Give examples from earlier in the book that show her lack of understanding or thought about reality.

2. Why have both despondency and hope left Edna after not seeing Robert?

Chapter XXXVI

Summary

When Edna is out walking, she often stops in a small quiet garden in the suburbs, where the proprietress sells and serves excellent food. It is not a place that is known to many people, and she never expects to see anyone she knows.

One afternoon, when she is eating dinner there, Robert walks in; he is uneasy and embarrassed when he sees Edna. Edna had intended to be reserved if she saw Robert but her reserve melts when she sees him. She asks him why he is staying away from her. Robert becomes almost angry and begs her to leave him alone.

Edna tells him he is selfish, not caring how she feels. Robert replies that she is being cruel, trying to force him into a disclosure that will result in nothing for him. They chat a bit about impersonal things; Robert tells Edna the end of the book she is reading so she won't have to finish it.

When they are finished, Robert walks Edna home. She goes into her room to wash up, and when she comes back to the living room, Robert is leaning back in a chair as if in a reverie. She leans over and kisses him, then moves away. Robert follows her and takes her in his arms. She touches his face with love and tenderness, and they kiss again.

Robert finally admits that he loves her. He says he has been fighting it because she was not free, but he had been dreaming of marrying her and that Leonce would set her free. Edna kisses him again and tells him he is being silly. She tells him she is not a

possession of Leonce's and that he could not set her free if he wanted to. She makes it clear that she gives herself as she chooses.

Robert turns white; he does not understand. Just then Adele's servant comes to the door to say that Adele is ready to have her baby and wants Edna to come. Robert kisses Edna good-bye with more passion than before. Edna tells him she loves him, and they can be together now. She asks him to wait for her until she returns from Adele's. Robert pleads with her not to go, but she leaves, promising to be back soon.

Analysis

Again Edna refuses to let Robert be. She presses until she gets a response. She tells Robert that he is being selfish, without thinking for a minute about how selfish she is being or how uncaring.

Edna is determined that her passion will win Robert over, and she is right at first. When she kisses him, he loses his senses and he kisses her back. Chopin lets us know that this is very different from the way she kisses Alcee. When she touches his face and presses his cheek against hers, "the action was full of love and tenderness." There's no question that Edna truly loves Robert; she has just blinded herself to the consequences of that love.

Robert finally admits that he loves her, but that he held back because she was not free to marry him, although he had dreamed of Leonce setting her free. Edna laughs at this because she has already set herself free. Robert, however, doesn't understand. He is a traditional Creole man and has no more understanding of Edna than Leonce or Alcee.

Robert begs Edna not to go to Adele's because he knows that without her there he will come to his senses and have to do the honorable thing. However, Edna, self-absorbed as ever, doesn't understand Robert any more than he understands her. She believes if they love each other, everything else will work out. As we have seen already, Edna lacks forethought. She prefers to live in her fantasy world.

Study Questions

1. Why does Robert call Edna "Mrs. Pontellier"?
2. Why is Edna being selfish when she calls Robert selfish?
3. Why is walking so important to Edna?

4. In what way does Robert show himself to be just like Leonce and Alcee?

5. What makes Robert finally tell Edna that he loves her?

6. Why was Robert fighting against his feelings?

7. What does Edna tell Robert about the state of her marriage?

8. Why does Robert turn white when he hears Edna's statement?

9. Why does Robert plead with Edna not to go to Adele's?

10. How do we know that Edna is living in her fantasy world?

Answers

1. He is trying to keep some distance between them.

2. All Edna thinks about anymore is her own pleasure and her own desires; she never stops to think of the turmoil Robert must feel being in love with a married woman.

3. Walking gives Edna a sense of independence and allows her to explore parts of life she would not ordinarily see.

4. Robert tells Edna the end of the book she is reading so she won't have to bother herself with finishing it; it's a very paternalistic attitude.

5. Edna kisses him and then moves away, and Robert follows her, takes her in his arms, and kisses her again. Then he finally has to tell her the truth.

6. Robert wanted Edna to be his wife, but he knew that she was not free and so he decided he better stay away.

7. She tells him that she is no longer one of Leonce's possessions and that she gives herself where she chooses. She says that she would laugh if Leonce offered to give her to Robert.

8. Robert is a traditional Creole man, and he doesn't understand Edna's attitude. If he did, he would disapprove.

9. Robert doesn't want the moment to end, because he knows that if he has time alone to come to his senses, he will have to do the honorable thing and leave.

10. Edna tells Robert that as long as they love each other

nothing else is of consequence. She still doesn't understand that there would be severe consequences to their union.

Suggested Essay Topics

1. How does Robert's attitude doom Edna's plans? Knowing what you know about Robert, would he allow Edna the independence she craves?

2. What would be the likely consequences if Edna decided to openly love Robert?

Chapter XXXVII

Summary

Edna arrives at the Ratignolles and finds Adele on a sofa in the salon, clearly in pain. She is berating Dr. Mandelet to her servant for being late. She is getting a little hysterical.

Finally Dr. Mandelet arrives, and Adele goes into her room. Edna stays with her, but she feels uneasy. She is recalling her own experiences with a feeling of dread. She begins to wish she had not come, but she stays. Although she is in agony, she stays to witness the birth that she considers a torture.

She is stunned and speechless when she says goodbye to Adele later. Adele is exhausted but whispers to Edna to think of her children.

Analysis

Adele is in obvious pain; her beautiful face is drawn and pinched, and her eyes are haggard and unnatural. We are clearly not supposed to look on this as a pleasant experience.

Edna begins to feel uneasy and afraid. There is a part of her that knows this childbirth will have some major impact on her. She doesn't remember much about her own childbirths because she was a different woman then. She remembers the stupor, which we know means that she felt hopeless and powerless when she gave birth.

Edna was in agony watching what she considered to be a scene

of torture; she has deep resentment against Mother Nature for forc-
ing women to bear children.

The last words Adele says to Edna are a plea to think of her
children. Although she didn't know it, this is what Edna had been
dreading. She couldn't witness a childbirth without thinking of her
own children, whom she had been trying very hard to forget.

Study Questions

1. What is Monsieur Ratignolle doing when Edna enters the
   drugstore?

2. How are the pains of childbirth first described as Edna sees
   Adele?

3. Why isn't Dr. Mandelet upset at Adele's "upraidings"?

4. What is the vague dread Edna began to feel?

5. Why do Edna's childbirths seem unreal and far away?

6. How would Edna explain the need for chloroform?

7. Why doesn't Edna leave when she wants to?

8. Why does Edna revolt against nature?

9. What are Adele's final words to Edna?

10. Does Edna think of her children that night?

Answers

1. He is mixing a painkiller for Adele.

2. Adele's face is drawn and pinched, and her eyes are haggard
   and unnatural.

3. Dr. Mandelet is used to women being hysterical right before
   they give birth.

4. Possibly, it was a foreshadowing of how this childbirth would
   affect her life.

5. Her children were born to her in her old life when she was a
   different woman; the woman she is today would not have
   children.

6. It is necessary to deaden both the physical and emotional pain of such a traumatic experience.

7. Edna is loyal to Adele.

8. Nature forced women to become mothers, whether they were emotionally equipped or not.

9. She pleads with her to think of the children.

10. No. She decides to postpone thinking about them until the following day.

Suggested Essay Topics

1. How would Edna and Adele differently describe childbirth?

2. Why is Adele so worried about Edna's children? What has she seen, heard or felt that would cause her to question Edna's commitment to her children?

Chapter XXXVIII

Summary

When Edna gets outside, she still feels dazed. Dr. Mandelet offers her a ride home, but she says she wants to walk. Dr. Mandelet decides to walk her home. He tells her that she shouldn't have been with Adele.

Edna responds that Adele was right, that she has to think of the children some time, preferably sooner than later. She tells Dr. Mandelet, in response to his question, that she will not be going abroad with Leonce when he returns. She tells him she just wants to be left alone and that nobody has the right to force her to do things, except children, maybe.

Dr. Mandelet seems to understand her. He says that youth is given to illusions, the illusions being the way to trap women into motherhood no matter what the consequences.

Edna agrees with Dr. Mandelet. She says her life had been a dream, but now she has awakened. She hints that she doesn't like what she found but thinks it is still probably better to wake up than to live with illusion all her life.

Dr. Mandelet offers his help if Edna feels like confiding in him, but she declines. She says the only thing she wants is her own way, which she realizes could cause pain to others. She also says she doesn't want to hurt her children.

When Edna returns home, she sits outside for a while, remembering her scene with Robert before she was called away. She acknowledges that tomorrow she will have to think of the children, but for tonight she just wants to be with Robert.

When Edna goes inside, Robert is not there. He left a note, saying he left because he loved her. Edna grows faint and lays down on the sofa. She remains there, not sleeping, all night.

Analysis

Edna is stung by Adele's words, and, against her will, she finally begins to think about the children. She had talked herself into believing that nobody, including her children, should have a claim on her, but now she's questioning that with regard to her children.

Dr. Mandelet seems to have some understanding of Edna's problem. He acknowledges that Nature secures mothers by allowing young girls to be swayed by illusion. He also acknowledges that not every woman is cut out for motherhood, or marriage, but that there is no escape once it has begun.

Edna agrees that her life was based on illusion before, and she says that even though she doesn't like reality, especially the fact that her children have to be considered, it's still better to know the truth than to live with illusion. Edna has awakened not to freedom but to limitation. She admits her selfishness, saying that she wants her own way and doesn't care who gets hurt—except that she doesn't want to hurt her children. This, as we know, is her central dilemma. How can she have Robert without hurting her children?

As upset as she is, all thoughts of the children leave Edna when she thinks about Robert waiting for her at her house. She is ready to put off thinking about them for one more day.

When Edna returns, Robert is gone. He cannot live the "free" life that Edna wants. He cannot live in sin or with scandal. Robert is an honorable Creole man and wants a traditional marriage.

Edna turned her "affair" with Robert into a fairy tale (see, for example, Chapter XIII). However in true fairy tales, the woman is awakened and worthy of love because she is pure, for example, Snow White, Cinderella, Rapunzel. In this case, Edna is not pure and is not worthy of Robert's love.

Study Questions

1. Why doesn't Edna want to go in Dr. Mandelet's car?

2. How do we know Edna is thinking about Robert?

3. Why are Edna's thoughts racing ahead of her?

4. Why does Dr. Mandelet think it was cruel of Adele to have had Edna there?

5. Why is Edna so confused?

6. How do we know that Dr. Mandelet has some understanding of Edna's problem?

7. How does Edna feel about her awakening?

8. How does Edna state the crux of her dilemma?

9. What happens when Edna begins to think about Robert again?

10. Why does Robert leave?

Answers

1. She wants to be alone with her thoughts.

2. The language is romantic: "the air was mild and caressing, but cool with the breath of spring and the night."

3. Edna is finally beginning to think about her children.

4. Dr. Mandelet believes that Edna is impressionable and not very stable, and he worries how she will be affected by what she saw and heard.

5. Edna had thought that even her children shouldn't affect what she wanted to do, but now she's beginning to wonder about that.

6. Dr. Mandelet acknowledges that not every woman is meant to be a mother.

7. Edna believes that even though she doesn't like what she

discovered about life, it is still better to know the truth than to be blinded by illusion.

8. Edna says that all she wants is her own way, even if she has to hurt some people, but she doesn't want to hurt her children.

9. She pushes the children out of her mind again and says she will think about them tomorrow.

10. Robert is an honorable man and cannot live the kind of life that Edna is suggesting; he wants a traditional marriage.

Suggested Essay Questions

1. How does Nature dupe women into becoming mothers?

2. Describe the central conflict in Edna's life, and how it would be different if it were the 1990s instead of the 1890s.

Chapter XXXIX

Summary

Back in Grand Isle, Victor is working and Mariequita is watching him. He is talking about the dinner at Edna's exaggerating every detail. Mariequita thinks he is in love with Edna, and she becomes jealous and sullen but then lets Victor reassure her.

To their surprise Edna appears before them, looking tired from her trip. She tells them she is just here for a rest and that any room will do. Then she asks what time dinner would be served.

Edna tells them her intention to go to the beach and take a swim. They warn her that the water is too cold, but she says she would dip her toes at least.

Edna walks down to the beach without thinking about anything in particular. She had thought all night, long after Robert left. She acknowledges that after Alcee she would find another lover, and she understood how this would affect Raoul and Etienne. She also understood clearly what she meant the day she told Adele she would never sacrifice herself for her children.

Edna became filled with despondence, realizing there was nothing and nobody she wanted except for Robert. She also realized that one day even that thought would fade, and she would be totally alone. Her children appeared before her like antagonists who were trying to enslave her, but she knew how to elude them.

All these things Edna thought about during her night on the couch. She isn't thinking of anything on her way to the beach. The voice of the sea is, as always, seductive. She sees a bird with a broken wing falling to the water.

Edna puts on her bathing suit but then takes it off, standing naked by the sea, feeling like a newborn creature. She walks into the water, into its sensuous touch. She keeps going, growing more tired. She thinks of Leonce and the children and how they thought they could possess her. She thinks that Mademoiselle Reisz would sneer, saying she is not a true artist because she does not possess a courageous soul.

Edna knows that Robert did not, and would not, understand her. She is far out now and feels that old moment of terror but it passes. She hears her father and sister's voices, and she hears the clanging spurs of the cavalry officer she had been infatuated with; finally she hears the hum of bees and smells the musty odor of pinks.

Analysis

This chapter opens with Victor exaggerating Edna's dinner party and her charms to the extent that Mariequita thinks of her as the "grand dame" of New Orleans. This is contrasted with the tired, defeated Edna who shows up at Grand Isle.

Critics debate over whether Edna's suicide was an act of passive defeat, an act of supreme courage, an acknowledgment that a woman seeking independence and selfhood has no viable alternatives in that society, or an acknowledgment that she doesn't have the psychological resources to resist the life society wants to foster on her. This is up to the reader to decide for him or herself.

Edna wasn't thinking on her way down to the beach because she was probably already in a hopeless stupor. She had been up all night thinking about what her life would be like if she stayed married for her children. She could have one affair after another, but she understood the effect that would have upon her children. She could end up married and alone, right back where she started. She refuses to give up what she had worked so hard for—her passion and independence.

If she didn't have children, she could just leave Leonce and do as she pleased. She knew there was no way to escape the "soul's slavery" her children put her into, except one.

Even if Edna were to leave Leonce, though, there is no other man out there who is any better. Both Alcee and Robert deny her independence as much as Leonce does. This contributes to Edna's feeling that she has no choice but to kill herself.

As Edna reaches the shore, she sees a bird with a broken wing heading back down to the water. This broken bird symbolizes her defeat. She has been broken by society and does not have the courage to fight anymore. And the seductive sea, as it has throughout the book, is calling her, offering rebirth and sensual pleasure. It is still the symbol of romantic possibility.

When Edna first thought about solitude and pictured the naked man on the beach, it was a sad picture. However, Edna feels "delicious" standing alone and naked by the sea. She is defeated, but there is some sense of power and freedom in the choice she is making. Nobody owns her anymore.

Of course it is questionable whether suicide is ever a true choice or just a passive giving up. Again it is up to the reader to decide.

Study Questions

1. What are Victor and Mariequita talking about when Edna shows up at Grand Isle?

2. Why, according to Mariequita, would it have been easy for her to run off with somebody's husband?

3. Why do Victor and Mariequita think Edna is an apparition when she first appears?

4. How does Edna seem when she first arrives?

5. Why isn't Edna thinking about anything as she walks down to the beach?

6. What has Edna concluded about her life?

7. What way has Edna devised to elude the slavery her children have planned for her?

8. What is the symbolism of the bird?

9. Why does Edna take her clothes off?

10. Why does Edna's old terror sink as quickly as it rises?

Answers

1. Victor is telling Mariequita, in exaggerated detail, about Edna's dinner party.

2. According to Mariequita it is the fashion to be in love with married people.

3. It is the middle of March, and there are never visitors to the island at that time.

4. She seems tired and indifferent. She doesn't care what room she has, all she asks for is some food.

5. Edna has been up all night thinking about her situation and deciding what to do.

6. Edna realizes that if she stayed married, she would continue to have affairs. She doesn't care about the scandal to herself or Leonce, but she realizes the effect it would have on her children and that she wouldn't be able to hurt them. She also realizes that she cannot live that way.

7. The only way Edna could avoid her fate was to kill herself.

8. The bird shows Edna's defeat; her wings are not strong enough to continue to fight, and the children are the reason.

9. She wants to feel completely free before she kills herself.

10. Edna is no longer afraid to die.

Suggested Essay Topics

1. Speaking as Edna, describe why you felt you had no choice but to kill yourself.

2. Was Edna's suicide an act of courage or defeat?

Sample Analytical Paper Topics

The following paper topics are based on the entire book. Following each topic is a thesis and sample outline. Use these as a starting point for your paper.

Topic #1

Although Edna thinks she will find true love and happiness with Robert, every single man in Edna's life has tried to control and/or repress her. Not one of them understands her need for independence.

How has each man in Edna's life attempted to control and/or repress Edna?

Outline

I. Thesis Statement: *None of the men in Edna's life understands her need for independence; they all try to control and/or repress her in some way.*

II. The Colonel, Edna's father, is a strict disciplinarian.

    A. Edna comes from a strict Presbyterian background.

    B. "Authority and coercion" are necessary to manage a wife.

III. Leonce Pontellier believes women should live only for their families' well-being.

    A.   It is the wife's place to look after the children.

    B.   He is courteous as long as Edna is submissive.

    C.   An artistic pasttime is all right as long as it doesn't interfere with family duties.

    D.   A wife has to act in ways that will be beneficial to her husband's business.

IV.   Alcee Arobin is a womanizer who knows how to take advantage.

    A.   He senses her latent sexuality and knows how to bring it out.

    B.   Once he has gotten her, he becomes proprietary and paternalistic.

V.   Robert Lebrun wants a traditional wife the same way Leonce does.

    A.   He tells Edna the end of the book she's reading so she doesn't have to bother finishing it.

    B.   He leaves when he realizes Edna doesn't want to marry him.

Topic #2

    Adele Ratignolle and Mademoiselle Reisz both are opposite ends of a spectrum, and both influence Edna's awakening and her final decision.

    How are the women different, and how has each woman affected Edna?

Outline

I.   Thesis Statement: *Adele Ratignolle and Mademoiselle Reisz are polar opposites, and both influence Edna in different ways.*

II.   Adele Ratignolle is a "mother-woman."

    A.   She is beautiful in a classic, very feminine way.

    B.   She has a baby every two years and is pregnant now.

    C.   She plays music to entertain her family and brighten her home.

III.   Mademoiselle Reisz is an artist.

    A.   She is small and ugly with an unpleasant personality.

    B.   She is unmarried and childless.

    C.   She plays piano for the love of art.

IV.   Adele wants Edna to be a better wife and mother.

    A.   She thinks Leonce should stay home more so he and Edna can spend more time together.

    B.   She reminds Edna to think of her children.

V.   Mademoiselle Reisz encourages Edna to be an artist.

    A.   She tells Edna that a true artist must have courage.

    B.   She helps Robert and Edna get together.

Topic #3

Chopin uses natural imagery in a romantic and sexual way to set the mood for her novel. What are some of the different images?

Outline

I.   Thesis Statement: *Chopin uses natural imagery in a romantic and sexual way to set the mood for her novel.*

II.   The sea is a symbol of romantic possibility.

    A.   The sea is seductive and sensuous.

    B.   The sea allows for limitless expansion.

    C.   The sea is a place of rebirth.

III.   Animals are sexual.

    A.   Edna is a beautiful, sleek animal waking up in the sun.

    B.   Edna's animalism responds to Victor's sexual story.

IV.   The moon shines a mysterious romantic light.

    A.   The moon takes away the weight of the darkness.

B.   The moon allows the spirit of the night to rise up.

C.   The moon allows Edna to hear clearly the voices of the night.

V.   Breezes, odors, and mists all speak sensually to Edna.

Topic #4

Edna's awakening takes many different forms. She awakens first to a vague dissatisfaction in her life, then to the freedom of sharing herself, to the passion of music, to the physical pleasure of swimming, to the sensual pleasure of her own body, to the intensity of true love, to the pleasure of solitude and independence, to sexual passion, and, finally, to limitation.

Describe the course of Edna's awakening.

Outline

I.   Thesis Statement: *Edna's awakening takes place over the course of the novel and includes several different smaller awakenings, usually of a sensual nature.*

II.   Edna awakens to a vague dissatisfaction with her life.

III. Edna awakens to the pleasure and freedom in sharing her thoughts.

IV.   Edna awakens to the passion of music.

V.   Edna awakens to the pleasure and freedom of swimming.

VI.   Edna awakens to the sensual pleasure of her own body.

VII. Edna awakens to the intensity of true love.

VIII. Edna awakens to the pleasure and necessity of solitude.

IX.   Edna awakens to sexual passion.

X.   Edna awakens to limitation.

SECTION FOUR

Bibliography

Quotations of *The Awakening* are taken from the following edition:

Chopin, Kate. *The Awakening*. New York: Avon Books, 1972.

Other Sources:

Dyer, Joyce. *The Awakening—A Novel of Beginnings*. New York: Twayne Publishers, 1993.

Koloski, Bernard, ed. *Approaches to Teaching Chopin's The Awakening*. New York: Modern Language Association of America, 1988.

Martin, Wendy, ed. *New Essays on The Awakening*. Cambridge: Cambridge University Press, 1988.

Skaggs, Peggy. *Kate Chopin*. Boston: Twayne Publishers, 1985.

Toth, Emily. *Kate Chopin*. New York: William Morrow & Co., Inc., 1990.

REA's Test Preps
The Best in Test Preparation

- REA "Test Preps" are far **more** comprehensive than any other test preparation series
- Each book contains up to **eight** full-length practice exams based on the most recent exams
- **Every** type of question likely to be given on the exams is included
- Answers are accompanied by **full** and **detailed** explanations

REA has published over 60 Test Preparation volumes in several series. They include:

Advanced Placement Exams (APs)
Biology
Calculus AB & Calculus BC
Chemistry
Computer Science
English Language & Composition
English Literature & Composition
European History
Government & Politics
Physics
Psychology
Spanish Language
United States History

College Level Examination Program (CLEP)
American History I
Analysis & Interpretation of Literature
College Algebra
Freshman College Composition
General Examinations
Human Growth and Development
Introductory Sociology
Principles of Marketing

SAT II: Subject Tests
American History
Biology
Chemistry
French
German
Literature

SAT II: Subject Tests (continued)
Mathematics Level IC, IIC
Physics
Spanish
Writing

Graduate Record Exams (GREs)
Biology
Chemistry
Computer Science
Economics
Engineering
General
History
Literature in English
Mathematics
Physics
Political Science
Psychology
Sociology

ACT - American College Testing Assessment

ASVAB - Armed Service Vocational Aptitude Battery

CBEST - California Basic Educational Skills Test

CDL - Commercial Driver's License Exam

CLAST - College Level Academic Skills Test

ELM - Entry Level Mathematics

ExCET - Exam for Certification of Educators in Texas

FE (EIT) - Fundamentals of Engineering Exam

FE Review - Fundamentals of Engineering Review

GED - High School Equivalency Diploma Exam (US & Canadian editions)

GMAT - Graduate Management Admission Test

LSAT - Law School Admission Test

MAT - Miller Analogies Test

MCAT - Medical College Admission Test

MSAT - Multiple Subjects Assessment for Teachers

NTE - National Teachers Exam

PPST - Pre-Professional Skills Tests

PSAT - Preliminary Scholastic Assessment Test

SAT I - Reasoning Test

SAT I - Quick Study & Review

TASP - Texas Academic Skills Program

TOEFL - Test of English as a Foreign Language

RESEARCH & EDUCATION ASSOCIATION
61 Ethel Road W. • Piscataway, New Jersey 08854
Phone: (908) 819-8880

Please send me more information about your Test Prep Books

Name _____

Address _____

City _____ State _____ Zip _____

Available at your local bookstore or order directly from us by sending in coupon below.

Available at your local bookstore or order directly from us by sending in coupon below.